William Halsey

This book was published in conjunction with an exhibition organized by the Greenville County Museum of Art, on view from May 5 through July 3, 1999.

Editor: Angela Gray Murphy

Designer: HansenDesignGroup

Photographers: Rick Rhodes and Blake Praytor

Greenville County Museum of Art
420 College Street
Greenville, SC 29601
864-271-7570

ISBN: 0-9603246-4-X

Printed in Hong Kong

frontispiece:
William Halsey, 1995
E.B. Hestor, Photographer

William Halsey

essay by Martha R. Severens

Greenville County Museum of Art
Greenville, South Carolina

William Halsey died in Charleston on February 14, 1999, while this publication was in production. We chose to preserve the content herein as originally written, because the artist was so vitally engaged in the processes of selecting the exhibition and writing its essay. For us, the creative spirit of William Halsey remains very much in the present tense.

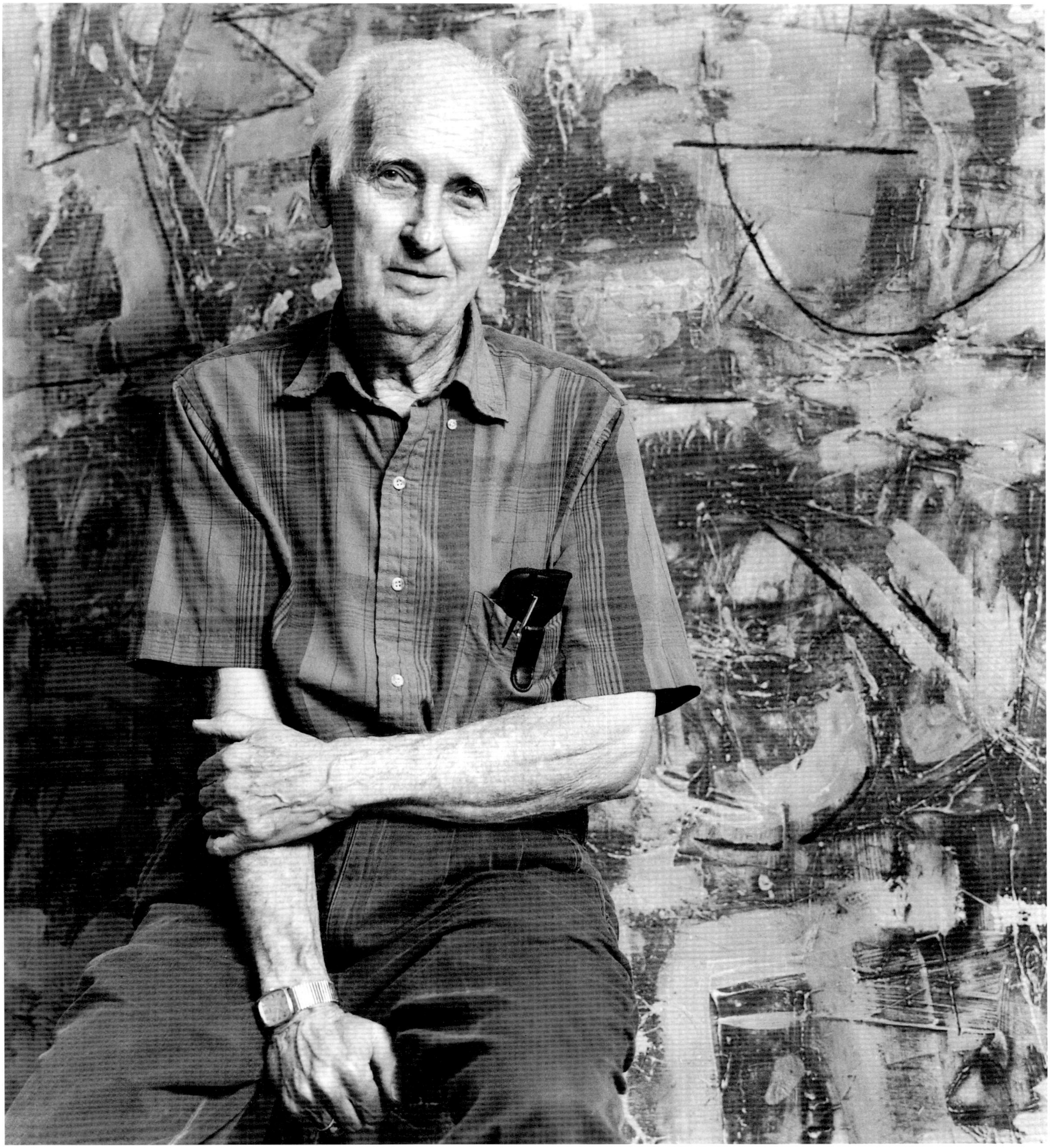

Introduction

The William Halsey exhibition is the second of three presentations to be held here in 1999 featuring important contemporary South Carolina artists. This triad—John Acorn, William Halsey, and Jeanet Dreskin—constitutes the Greenville County Museum's contribution to the South Carolina Arts Commission's millennial celebration, *Views from the Edge of the Century.*

In her groundbreaking project, *The Charleston Renaissance*, Curator Martha R. Severens, who admirably produced this exhibition and publication as well, appropriately positioned Halsey as the singular link between Charleston's cultural renewal and the subsequent dawning of a new era for the arts across the state. Indeed, culturally speaking, it might be argued that during the immediate decades after World War II, South Carolina, without Halsey, could have claimed to be little more than the nostagically entrenched bastion of Secession and the eagerly abandoned childhood home of Jasper Johns. Halsey almost singlehandedly guarded the modernist flame for years here before the rest of the state was finally drawn to its light. For this alone we should be grateful, but there is one thing more—in the process he became one of the finest painters in the country.

I have known very few artists of William Halsey's caliber. I regret that it took us so long to meet, but I am thankful for the extraordinary opportunity of rummaging with him through his treasure-trove of a studio. His has been an astoundingly productive career, and his example as an artist/educator sets the highest standards of personal creativity and generosity. William Halsey is the epitome of what it means to be an artist: he is an inspiration.

Otto Rank wrote that "the redeeming power of art . . . resides in the way in which it lends concrete existence to abstract ideas of the soul." In this spirit Halsey has surrounded himself with the mirrors of his work. Through a kind of aesthetic archeological alchemy he revitalizes the ancient fragments of human effort. He wills the shards and glyphs to rise up out of the ruins and dance—to shout hallelujahs for having once lived while living still.

Thomas W. Styron
Director
Greenville County Museum of Art

Acknowledgments

Primacy of place belongs to the artist himself who has been most generous with his time and has given free access to his archives and to his work. Next is Corrie McCallum, a distinguished artist in her own right and Halsey's wife since 1939, who has contributed her own recollections and perceptions. Their son, David Halsey, has been of tremendous logistical assistance throughout and deserves a special note of thanks.

Tom Styron, director of the Greenville County Museum of Art, choreographed the selection of works for the exhibition, to the delight and surprise of the artist. Sandi Rupp, director of the Hampton III Gallery, deserves special recognition as the individual who introduced the artist to Tom Styron and who has cheerfully facilitated the project in many ways. Mark Sloan, director of the Halsey Gallery at the College of Charleston, has also furnished ideas and interns who have been of great help.

William Halsey's many friends, admirers, and students have come forward with their tributes and recollections: Dr. William H. Gerdts, who has authored the thoughtful appreciation, and, in addition, Merton Simpson, Brian Rutenberg, Johnson Hagood, and Casimer Kowalski. Lenders to the exhibition: the College of Charleston, the Columbia Museum of Art, Dr. and Mrs. Ambrose Hampton, Thomas M. Cooper, Jr. and Mr. and Mrs. Dennis R. Tavernetti have been most generous and accommodating.

The Museum gratefully acknowledges support for the publication of the catalogue from the Museum Association, Mr. and Mrs. Dennis R. Tavernetti, BBA Nonwovens, and an anonymous donor. *William Halsey* is a collaborative project with the South Carolina Arts Commission and NationsBank. Special funding is provided by the National Endowment for the Arts.

Martha R. Severens
Curator
Greenville County Museum of Art

An Appreciation

Bill Halsey has remained Charleston's most celebrated resident painter ever since I had the pleasure and honor to meet him and become both an admirer and a friend many decades ago. Though his art is not unknown beyond his native city, the question might be asked why Bill is not a painter of greater national renown. Frankly, I can't easily identify the reasons for that situation, though his remove from New York, the center of the American art world in the twentieth century, is certainly a factor. Nor do I wish to hypothesize what might have befallen Bill had he settled in the nation's artistic center, which he considered perhaps more than once during his career. But I can assure the citizenry of South Carolina that they are far better off for Bill's continued presence there.

It was easy to arrive at this conclusion, because, through the years of my sustained acquaintance with Bill, I have become aware of the importance of an established artistic presence in cultural centers beyond New York. I met Bill in Charleston late in 1953—forty-five years from when I am writing this "appreciation"—and that's quite a long period of time. I realized very quickly—from the quality and diversity of his artistic achievement even then, from all I learned of him at the time from other Charlestonians, and from the brilliance and perceptivity of his persona—that he was the most gifted artist in South Carolina. I was also tremendously fortunate that Bill, and his equally talented wife, Corrie McCallum, immediately became good friends of mine, and that friendship has endured even while their own artistry has never ceased to grow and develop, with their achievements remaining of the highest order.

As an art historian of earlier American paintings, I do not usually deal with artists face to face. But every once in a while I've formed friendships with contemporary artists, and I must admit it's usually been extremely rewarding, even though my expectations have been high in that regard. Well, I guess they ought to be, because Bill Halsey was the *first* professional painter with whom I developed rapport. As both artist and friend, Bill immediately engendered the standards which I value tremendously to this day. Charleston and South Carolina ought to be very, very grateful that he stayed.

William H. Gerdts
Professor of Art History
The Graduate School and University Center
The City University of New York
December 1998

I was born in Charleston and came back here because I felt strongly that there were too many artists in a few areas and too few artists in small cities and towns and that I could be vastly more useful in my native state than any place else. If there was a more general distribution of creative artists working in smaller communities, there would be a wider interest in and understanding of contemporary art in this country. I plan to continue my work and teaching here and the growth of my own painting and thinking will have more than an individual meaning, since it will make my influence and instruction of greater value.

William Halsey, 1952

William Halsey and the Fabric of Charleston

A native Charlestonian, William Halsey has spent almost his entire career a few blocks from where he was born. Halsey's preference for abstraction, however, separates him from the artistic tradition of Charleston, long-steeped in conventional realism. Unlike the artists who preceded him, especially the leading spirits of the Charleston Renaissance, Halsey has not made alluring pictures of the city. Instead, he uses Charleston, its colors, textures, and geometry, as inspiration. While not picturing Charleston, he incorporates the city's essence in his materials and in the well-worked surfaces of his art. In some instances, he literally takes the component parts from his surroundings; this is particularly true in his constructions where he has employed weathered boards, old balusters, keys, hooks, and buckles–the detritus of his urban situation. But even in his collages and the more recent oil-stick paintings there is an energy, a passion, and a radiant color that evoke the city as it is today. After all, Halsey remains a Charlestonian, and his abstractions intimately reflect his hometown.

In the early 1950s, while affiliated with Manhattan's Bertha Schaefer Gallery, Halsey could have opted to settle in New York, which was just then emerging as the capital of the art world. He deliberately chose to stay in his birthplace. While some of his reasons were economic and pragmatic–such as raising three children–perhaps deep down he recognized that his art was and is intimately tied to what has been called "America's Most Historic City."

Despite his focus on Charleston, Halsey has succeeded in countering any charge of provincialism; he has traveled extensively, but not necessarily to the mainstream art centers of the Western world. Rather, he has taken his pens and sketchpads to such exotic destinations as the Yucatan, Honduras, Tahiti, and Morocco. But often he sees these distant places through a Charleston-colored lens:

> Growing up in a Charleston impoverished and neglected, surrounded by flaking plaster, mortarless brick walls, old tiles, and rotting wood, I saw them as delight rather than decay. Ever since, I have carried on a love affair with fragments, shards, ruins, bits of past civilizations. This is not simply nostalgia. A large part of it is visual-tactile pleasure derived from color, broken edges, worn surfaces produced by time and weather. The enigmatic quality of things not quite complete, the mystery of symbols not entirely understood. Later, when I traveled, I developed an enthusiasm for Maya culture, saw Egyptian wall paintings, Etruscan ceramics, African sculpture, Peruvian textiles, the stones of Machu-Picchu. To me they were at the same time excitingly dissimilar and very much related, and I related them to the Charleston of my childhood. So, the more I have traveled, the further I have gone, the more I have come back to the same place and person.[1]

Halsey's artistic beginnings were precocious. His mother, Eleanor Loeb Halsey, recognized his penchant for drawing and encouraged this pastime. She showed a selection to Elizabeth O'Neill Verner who became the youth's first instructor and mentor. One of the leading artists of the Charleston Renaissance, Verner studied at the Pennsylvania Academy of the Fine Arts. As a self-supporting Charleston artist, she served as a role model for the young Halsey.

Edward I. R. Jennings, one of the few Charleston artists who embraced modernism, provided another artistic example. In the early 1920s Jennings studied at Columbia University, New York, with Arthur Wesley Dow, a champion of aesthetics over subject matter. Dow emphasized purity of form and design, color harmony, and the craft of making art. Jennings, who taught Halsey informally in his Confederate Home studio, served as a conduit of modernist theory.

After graduation from high school, Halsey attended the University of South Carolina in Columbia for two years. While there he concentrated on courses in arts and humanities. He became active in the local theater, painting stage sets for such productions as *Red Riding Hood*, *Anna Christie*, and *The Mikado*. He pursued his interest in art at a summer workshop in Maine and in Greenville with Margaret Moore Walker. Wrestling with applications for art schools, he seriously considered the Art Students League in New York and Yale University. Asked for her advice, Verner responded:

> I think the best thing I can think of for you is to stay in Charleston for one year and work out your salvation here. I do not know of any artists in New York who have been more successful than the Charleston group and by this I do not speak of myself but of Edward von Siebold Dingle, Alice Ravenel Huger Smith, Anna Heyward Taylor, Alfred Hutty and others. You would in no way rival or conflict with any of this group but to my mind would be a great addition to it. . . . I think very often we make the mistake of going too far afield.[2]

Halsey solicited additional counsel from Laura M. Bragg, a Northerner who had headed the Charleston Museum for twenty years. In this capacity, Bragg witnessed and contributed to the city's cultural renewal, until her departure in 1930 to become the director of the Berkshire Museum in Massachusetts. Halsey wrote to her about his aspirations:

> I want somebody who will not so much instruct me, tell me *what to do*, as help me to do *what I want to do*. I need primarily a great deal of work from the nude model, just ground-work in draughtmanship, and contact with real artists, modern artists who know what's going on in the world of art. For Charleston, though I love her very much as a city, is, as you know, still practically in the china painting era, as far as art is concerned. I don't want to be influenced by other artists, imitate the popular advanced methods, but I want to see what's going on, get a thorough foundation, and then come back and work out my own method for myself. Whether I'm modernist, non-objective, or realist, I want to say what I've got to say in my own way. Perhaps I haven't anything to say yet, but I believe I will have something some day.[3]

Ultimately, Halsey chose the School of the Museum of Fine Arts in Boston at the suggestion of Serge Soudekine, the set designer for DuBose Heyward's and George Gershwin's *Porgy and Bess*. The Museum School, a respected institution, stressed a traditional and academic curriculum. Halsey's primary instructors were Alexandre Iacovleff, Karl Zerbe, and Lewis Rubinstein. Zerbe, born in Germany, had pursued a traditional academic program in Munich and Paris, and Rubinstein had studied in Paris with Fernand Léger and Amedée Ozenfant. While Iacovleff stressed drawing, Zerbe revolutionized the curriculum by emphasizing color and individual expression.[4] Halsey studied such conventional subjects as anatomy, perspective, composition, and drawing, and regularly attained A-level grades. He learned a variety of painting techniques, but tended to emphasize fresco, a medium popularized by the New Deal art programs. By his last year he was sufficiently proficient in fresco that he was asked to teach it at the school.

Halsey's interest in murals and fresco was further fostered by an eighteen-month sojourn in Mexico made possible by a Paige Fellowship awarded by the Museum School. Designed to supplement the curriculum in Boston, the purpose of the fellowship was to send aspiring students to Europe. Because war threatened Europe during the summer of 1939, Zerbe encouraged Halsey, with his young bride, Corrie McCallum, to go to Mexico instead. Zerbe urged that they leave as soon as possible, before the committee returned from summer break to overturn this change in destination.

Reflecting upon this dramatic and sudden modification of the fellowship, Halsey now sees it as an act of fate. He believes that if they had gone to Europe, they would have spent all their time in museums looking at old masters. In Mexico they did not find "great collections of world painting, but Mexican regional art, weaving and an emphasis on ceramics." There was also the scenery and the architecture, and most of all, color. "The kind of color I use is strong or primitive, intense color–something very present in Mexico, not present in Europe."[5]

Despite his misgivings about Charleston, Halsey briefly returned there in mid-1941 at the conclusion of the Paige Fellowship. During his absence, the Gibbes Art Gallery had mounted a one-man exhibition of his work, the first of many he would have there. It circulated to Norfolk and Lynchburg, Virginia, and was the beginning of an impressive series of regular solo and group exhibitions that has continued throughout his career. In 1942 his work was featured in an exhibition at the Telfair Academy in Savannah, Georgia, where he was working as the art school director. The following year, he took a job at the Southeastern Shipyard Corporation in Savannah, and at the end of the war, Halsey moved home to Charleston permanently.

In the ten years he spent away from Charleston, both the artist and the city had grown. Halsey had acquired the drawing skills and fundamentals that he had sought, and his horizons had been broadened through travel. He had begun his teaching career, a mainstay of his life that would continue for forty years until his retirement from the College of Charleston in 1984. While much about Charleston had remained the same, the presence of the Navy Base had transformed the economy of the region and population in the area had exploded.

For over fifty years William Halsey and Corrie McCallum have made Charleston their home. In addition to raising three children, they have forged an exemplary artistic partnership of mutual support and constructive criticism. As he says, "Neither one of us would have made it, under the circumstances, without the other."[6] They have had studios under the same roof, taught at the same schools, exhibited jointly and separately, and have often traveled together. From their travels they developed paintings, and in 1971 they cooperated on the publication, *A Travel Sketchbook*, which reveals their different reactions to foreign lands.

As teachers, the Halseys have been an important force in the community. William Halsey's earliest affiliation was with the Gibbes Art Gallery, the city's art museum. Halsey directed the Gibbes School, using two large rooms at the rear of the first floor as classrooms. In 1953, after a disagreement with director Robert N. S. Whitelaw, Halsey, McCallum, and Willard Hirsch established the Charleston Art School. By 1958 they were conducting classes for as many as 160 students in a variety of subjects ranging from drawing the nude figure to painting and sculpture.

One exceptional student was Merton Simpson, who has achieved an international reputation as an artist and art dealer specializing in African art. Because he is an African-American, Simpson was never formally enrolled in any of Halsey's classes, but the two artists have had a rewarding relationship since the mid-1940s. As Halsey recalled:

> There was no place for a black student to go for art instruction then. Merton was introduced to me by artist Jean Robinson Fleming, who had seen his work and thought that I could help him. He started bringing his work around to my studio, and I would critique it. He was never officially in any of my studio classes at the Gibbes, or anywhere else for that matter, because it just wasn't allowed. . . . Merton always found a way to be around art. If he couldn't get in the front door at the Gibbes, he did odd jobs at the back. He also worked for a frame shop after school.[7]

Simpson went on to study art at New York University with William Baziotes and at the Cooper Union Art School with Robert Gwathmey. He met distinguished figures such as Romare Bearden and Hale Woodruff, and was included in exhibitions at the Metropolitan Museum of Art and the Guggenheim Museum. Despite his success, however, Simpson has remained loyal to his mentor. He has recently written: "For over sixty years William Halsey has been for me an artistic titan. He has always been there whenever I needed him. He always had the special ability to say so much by saying just the few right words."[8]

Simpson, in turn, has contributed to Halsey's art, introducing him to African textiles. Halsey remembers, "I was intrigued . . . I loved them . . . not just because they are beautiful, [but because I] really had a feeling of their origin and . . . the mystery of Africa."[9] One resulting work, *Double Congo Doors*, (page 51) is a large-scale collage composed of cut and torn scraps of African textiles combined with old paint rags used by the artist. It represents a synthesis of Simpson's cultural roots with Halsey's fascination with folk creativity.

Other Halsey students have prospered, including Brian Rutenberg, who also resides in New York. Having studied at the College of Charleston during the early 1980s, Rutenberg credits Halsey with imparting an appreciation for "the subtle discordances and gradual harmonies that go into constructing a painting, [lessons that] have remained with me to this day."[10]

Perhaps Halsey's legacy is manifested most emphatically in Charleston, however, where former students such as Casimer Kowalski continue to live and work. Kowalski teaches art for middle and high school students at the Charleston School of the Arts. In the mid-1980s Kowalski served as Halsey's studio assistant, helping primarily with the large freestanding constructions, such as *Shaman II* (page 55), cutting wood and coordinating the fabrication of the metal pieces with a welder. Now, with his own students, Kowalski says that he tries to "return the guidance, knowledge, and compassion," that Halsey shared with him.[11]

Much of Halsey's work is material autobiography; *Nail, Spike, and Copper Tube* (page 59), for example, was inspired by a board he constructed to hang his keys on. *White Counterpoint* reflects his fondness for wood scraps, which may have its origins in the Halsey Lumber Yard, a family business. Collages such as *Denim* (page 71) incorporate actual remnants of Halsey's own wardrobe–worn, paint-splattered, well-used shirts and pants. Many of the early paintings portray nocturnal streetscapes. The artist enjoys walking the streets at night, not only because in the summer it is cooler, but also because of the mood: "Everything looks more exotic at night, night light, exciting, more mystery, camouflage."[12] He frequently captures this drama when he includes a lurking silhouette in a window, as in *Blue Grille* (page 25).

In the early 1960s Halsey completed a series of heavily textured paintings that featured a simple chair form (page 39). He associates the old, wooden chair with his mother. Eleanor Halsey was the first to recognize her son's talents, and fostered his early schooling with Elizabeth Verner. After listing his mother's many civic accomplishments and acknowledging her thirty-year career as executive director of the Charleston County Tuberculosis Association, Halsey paid her the following tribute:

> When I was sure of little else, I never doubted her love, her strength, her faith. She could, and did, criticize me, but she brooked no criticism from others. She was the Rock of Gibraltar, the iron fist in the velvet glove. A small, lovely lady who managed to be Victorian in many ways, and at the same time avant-garde in her tolerance, in the pioneer work she did for better health care, for social reform, for education. Though she had no particular artistic background or inclination, she helped me to be an artist, because if that was what I wanted to be, that was what she wanted me to be.[13]

For Halsey, the chair assumed associations that transcended its mundane nature. He was not the first artist to use an empty chair and endow it with personal meaning. Vincent van Gogh, who Halsey admits is an inspiration, repeatedly used a simple slat-back chair–similar in design to Halsey's–as a subject, most notably in his well-known painting of his bedroom in Arles.

Pressed to list others whose work he admires, Halsey cites Pablo Picasso, Henri Matisse, Paul Klee, and Jean Dubuffet. Picasso's invention of collage and whimsical sculptures created with found objects–such as a bull's head from a bicycle seat–have direct parallels in Halsey's oeuvre. The rich, sonorous colors of Matisse find correspondences in the Charlestonian's paintings, collages, and sculptures. Among Halsey's favorite hues is an intense red, evident in such works as *Red Orbit* (page 33), *Magic Carpet* (page 69), and *Metamorphosis* (page 77). Klee's tendency to draw over layers of color with his own visual vocabulary of markings is mirrored in Halsey's large, multi-paneled *Stones of Time* (pages 45-47). In *Moon Door* (page 54), the translucent, ethereal blue is reminiscent of similar tones that recur in Klee's work. Halsey's fondness for textures, not just of fabric but of paint, to which he has added such gritty substances as sand and marble dust, resembles Dubuffet's heavily encrusted surfaces.

Much of Halsey's work is in tune with anonymous creators: African weavers, Mayan sculptors, Native American craftsmen, and even graffiti artists. In his studio, he keeps a group of black-and-white photographs of Charleston's sidewalk graffiti, which his friend Bill Jordan took around 1976. In addition to the self-consciously amusing "Oh, Boy! Wet cement!" some of these feature long cracks and numbers scratched into sidewalks, not unlike the surface articulation Halsey has worked into *Totemic* (page 63), *Shaman* (page 61), and the freestanding steel *Shaman II* (page 55).

Occasionally, like Pop artists Andy Warhol and James Rosenquist, Halsey found inspiration for subject matter in newspapers and magazines. In his striking painting *Hanged Men* (page 43), for example, Halsey worked from a *New York Times* photograph of two Jewish men executed in Baghdad. Based on this clipping, which he tacked up in his studio, he made a series of broad line drawings of the figures' silhouettes. When he translated them into the large-scale painting he retained their postures and their haunting floating quality but eliminated the signs that hung around their necks, creating a more timeless and universal image of social horror.

Although they are often evocative, Halsey's titles offer few direct insights into the interpretation of his pieces. Halsey admits laboring over titles, so much so that he keeps a set of index cards with interesting words gleaned from the dictionary. Many of the most suggestive titles conjure associations with distant cultures. The shaman, for example, is often an outsider with special powers who mediates or has special visionary capabilities. In this way Halsey introduces a reference to himself, connecting the artist with the shaman. In others, such as *Denim* (page 71), the self-referential title is more overt: the collage consists of old work clothes the artist once wore.

Halsey has said, "collage is my favorite process; [it's the] process of using things acquired over time."[14] Similarly, his collages were deliberately built up as successive layers dried. He went through gallons of glue and most often tore his fabric rather than cut it. As demonstrated in both *Red Orbit* (page 33), and *Red Earth, Yellow Moon* (page 35), Halsey revels in rough and frayed edges, ragged surfaces and ridges, creating topographic tactility. Often he finishes with an overall oil wash of color, which serves to harmonize the composition.

Typically, Halsey makes his collages on the floor, working from above. Like the more notorious Jackson Pollock, Halsey moves around, neither forcing a vertical nor horizontal orientation on his composition. His choice of four-feet-square sheets of Masonite is ideal for this purpose; not only do they provide a firm surface on which to work, but the square format is open-ended. "When it's square it's all even . . . a lot of squares started with no top or bottom; I could turn them every which way, sort of a different challenge from the usual, whether horizontal/landscape or vertical/figure, depends on what you do."[15]

In 1989 Roberta Kefalos of the Gibbes Museum of Art described Halsey's working method:

> He builds up a ground of varied surfaces and textures with gesso, sand and marble dust, blocking out forms and shapes with stencils and tape. Over this, he washes and blends oil paint to achieve a composition of richly-modulated colors and abstract images which emerge from the saturation of paint on the textured surface. As in much of his work, Halsey values the random flow of colors and unpredictable, accidental effects that result from this process of painting.[16]

Although he has occasionally tried acrylic paint, Halsey's preference is for oil. His ability to exploit the textural properties of oil paint has been a lifelong talent, beginning as early as the late 1930s with his Mexican paintings, when he animated their surfaces with heavy impasto. Halsey dislikes the housekeeping required by brushes and tends instead to use ordinary kitchen implements, such as spatulas, or tools more often used by carpenters, such as screwdrivers and pliers. In recent years his preferred medium has been oil-stick, which he applies to heavily textured paper. Using a smaller, more manageable format, he still prefers to work on a flat surface, frequently moving his paper around to suit his needs.

Early in his career Halsey had several mural commissions–at the Berkshire Museum, the Dock Street Theatre and the Sears and Roebuck building in Charleston, and a synagogue in Baltimore. These occurred just as government sponsorship of public art was coming to an end and as avant-garde New York artists were reverting to painting on canvas. In an article aimed at architects, the artist bemoaned the lack of mural opportunities: "Murals, unlike easel paintings, cannot be conceived in isolated units. To have integrity they must be part of an architectural whole. To be part of an architectural whole, they must be part of an architect's original plan."[17] Despite the lack of such commissions, Halsey still managed to allude to mural-like qualities in his art: beyond their large scale, many paintings and collages resemble the scumbled and irregular surfaces of old stucco and the peeled paint layers found in old buildings.

While Halsey favored Masonite as a support from early in his career, in the 1980s he began to use prefabricated doors for both his paintings and collages, indulging his passion for large formats. In almost all instances, he has used them as verticals, as they were originally intended. Occasionally he has retained the memory of the door in his titles, as in *Moon Door* (page 54) or *Double Congo Doors* (page 51). *River Gods* (page 57) also consists of two narrow vertical panels, separated by a two-inch interval. This allows its cutout contours and interior perforations to read dynamically as negative and positive shapes.

This three-dimensional interplay and the tension between a manipulated surface and volumetric form are essential to several freestanding works. In the mid-1980s, Halsey made preliminary drawings that his studio assistant fabricated with a jigsaw. The end results, as exemplified by *Two-Faced Graffiti God #1* (page 48) and *Grandfather*, are two-sided hybrids of sculpture and painting, rather than sculptures fully realized in the round. Their surfaces are integrated by color and incised designs reminiscent of hieroglyphs, and the forms and shallow spaces shift, expand, and attenuate as the viewer moves around them.

Characteristic of much of Halsey's work is his tendency to layer materials as well as ideas. In the heavily textured collages of his middle period, as well as the late oil-sticks, he has often laid down a surface to which he repeatedly returns and reworks. Sometimes years intervene before he revisits them, at times obliterating and/or re-orienting a work. An outgrowth of his natural frugality perhaps, this reworking also relates to his fascination with layers of history, mirrored in his favorite locales, Charleston and Mexico. Sometimes even titles change: *Voodoo, Violet, and Blue* (page 29) was once *Romanesque*. The earlier designation makes clear its architectural associations, while the final title evokes something both mysterious and humorous. *Metamorphosis* (page 77) is literally that: begun in 1985, the artist has reworked it twice, first in 1991 and then in 1998. As in the sculptures, he introduces an integrating, calligraphic design, here in green and white gestures that resemble sidewalk graffiti.

Halsey's fondness for "things with a past"–whether in his paintings or assembled sculptures, discarded paint rags or African textiles, Mayan ruins or Charleston–is one of the several leitmotifs of his career. "Frayed edges, worn materials; worn surfaces associated with Charleston; Charleston is different materials."[18] For many years, he has worked intuitively and organically, as he admits: "I like to feel that as I paint, the painting begins to have a life of its own; it becomes, and it demands certain things. I work with it, and I fight with it. Eventually there comes a resting place, a unity, an entity. The painting has become a thing complete on its own, inevitable."[19]

Reflecting upon his place in the community Halsey recently ruminated: "Nobody here was impressed. In ways it was lonely. We did make a living here, but we felt isolated. This was a natural condition at the time–I was different and peculiar."[20] To alleviate the sense of isolation as well as the drudgery of routine, both Halsey and McCallum traveled extensively, sometimes together, sometimes with friends. Travel was their "escape mechanism."

Halsey has also felt the lack of a supportive artistic community. Although he was one of very few avant-garde artists in the state, for years he and McCallum were nonetheless active in the South Carolina Artists' Guild. They also regularly participated in regional juried exhibitions. Despite his two decades at the College of Charleston he never felt there was much collegiality or significant interchange among faculty. In 1968 he commented on the art scene in Charleston:

> There are a lot of people who paint in Charleston, but there aren't many artists. People in Charleston don't want contemporary art. They want the same paintings that their fathers hung on the wall, and the same furniture. An artist really shouldn't try to make a living in Charleston because there really hasn't been much of a market for contemporary art here, although it is improving.

Thirty years later he offered the following assessment: "That's the kind of place I live in. I thought I was changing it–but I realize I wasn't a bit."[21] Regardless, Halsey has forged on. By maintaining a presence in his native city, by exhibiting and teaching there, Halsey has sustained a vital connection with the larger world of modern art. Charleston is now home to numerous galleries and exhibition venues. The Spoleto Festival USA and a burgeoning tourist industry have fueled its art activities. Nevertheless, the predominant taste continues to prefer the picturesque, much as when Halsey began his career. Halsey continues to pursue his own vision: "For years I vacillated. I was undecided. I like people to like what I do–to have a public; so I tried to do, for example, Charleston street scenes, local scenes. Then I reached a point: to hell with that! I like to paint what I like. Color and space and shape. Now I enjoy it more."[22] Perhaps Elizabeth Verner, Halsey's first instructor, was prescient in her exhortation to him sixty-five years ago to "work out your salvation here."

Works of Art & Commentary

NIGHT HOUSES, 1951

By a good margin, the outstanding painting in the show is from the brush of a newcomer, William Halsey. All sorts of superlative adjectives could be invoked to describe his *Night Houses*, a crisp, knowing semi-abstraction with the suavest of color relationships.

Alonzo Lansford, 1948

At the Bertha Schaefer [Gallery], there's the first local one-man exhibition of paintings by William Halsey. These are mostly landscapes . . . done in a style whose emphasis on flat-pattern, two-dimensional development gives the artist a good chance to deploy his feeling for vivid color and effective design. I especially admired . . . *Night Houses*, with its moonlit façades.

Robert M. Coates, 1951[23]

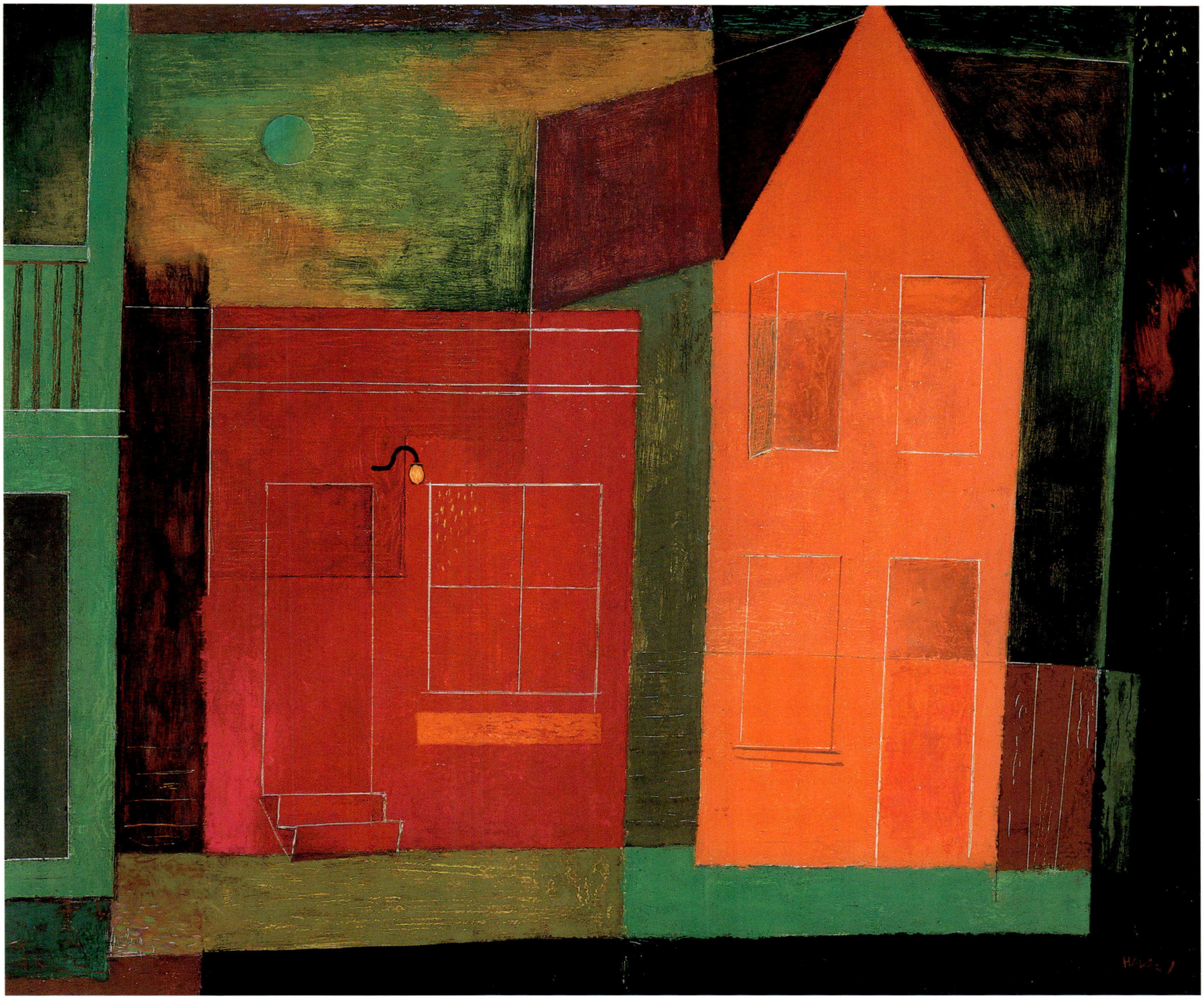

END OF TOWN, 1953

William Halsey's work at the Bertha Schaefer Gallery is a pleasant reminder of the worth of reality to an artist who has the gift to enliven it with feeling. Many of his paintings are of effects, in themselves poetically enjoyable–such as the shimmer of life in an aquarium, or the suggested moon glow upon building façades. This artist affects no more nor less than a studied simplification of his material, passing over complexity in order to achieve a direct and disciplined abstracting. But what he communicates is distinguished by a sensitive approach to painting itself and by effects of pleasing and imaginative color.

Carlyle Burrows, 1951[24]

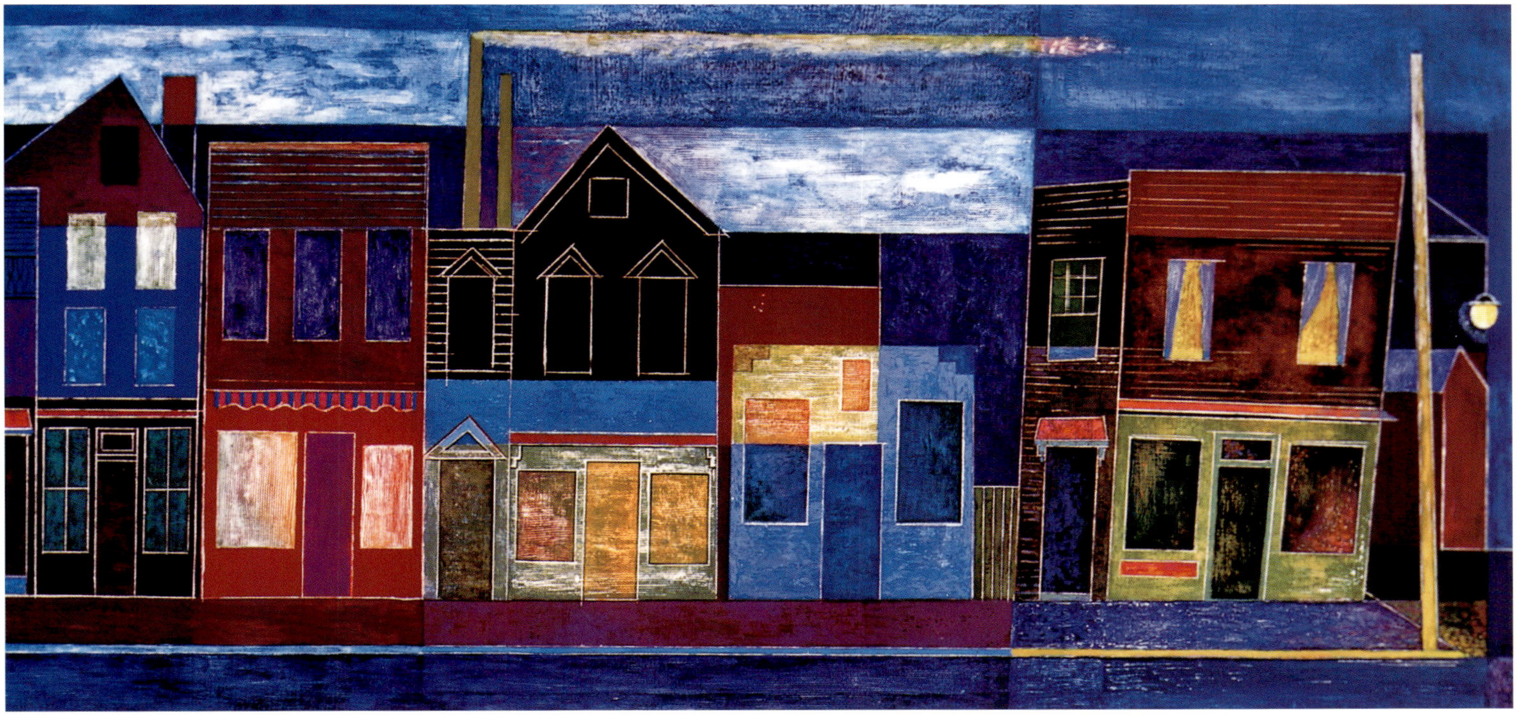

Blue Grille, 1956

Halsey has spent most of his career in Charleston, at first as a matter of necessity and then as a conscious choice. There his sense of place has proved to be a sustaining force in his life and work. Until recently he enjoyed the notoriety of being the city's only modern painter. In this isolated setting, the artist developed his own style at his own pace. Although he gradually earned a national reputation, Halsey has never felt compelled to make concessions to artistic vogues. As he neatly puts it, "I've always worked on the wrong things, at the wrong time and in the wrong place."

Anthony F. Janson, 1978[25]

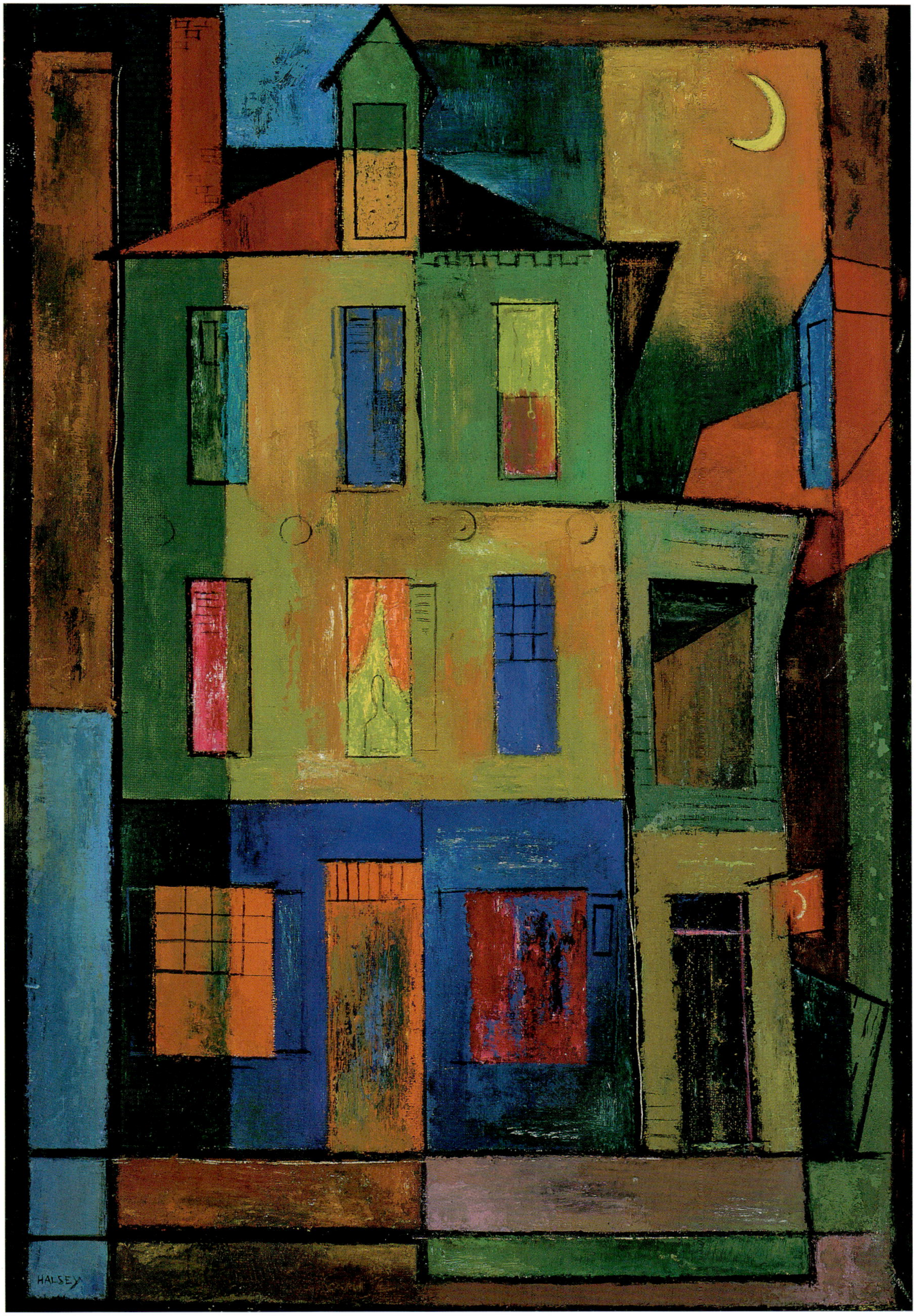
HALSEY

FROM OUTER SPACE, 1964

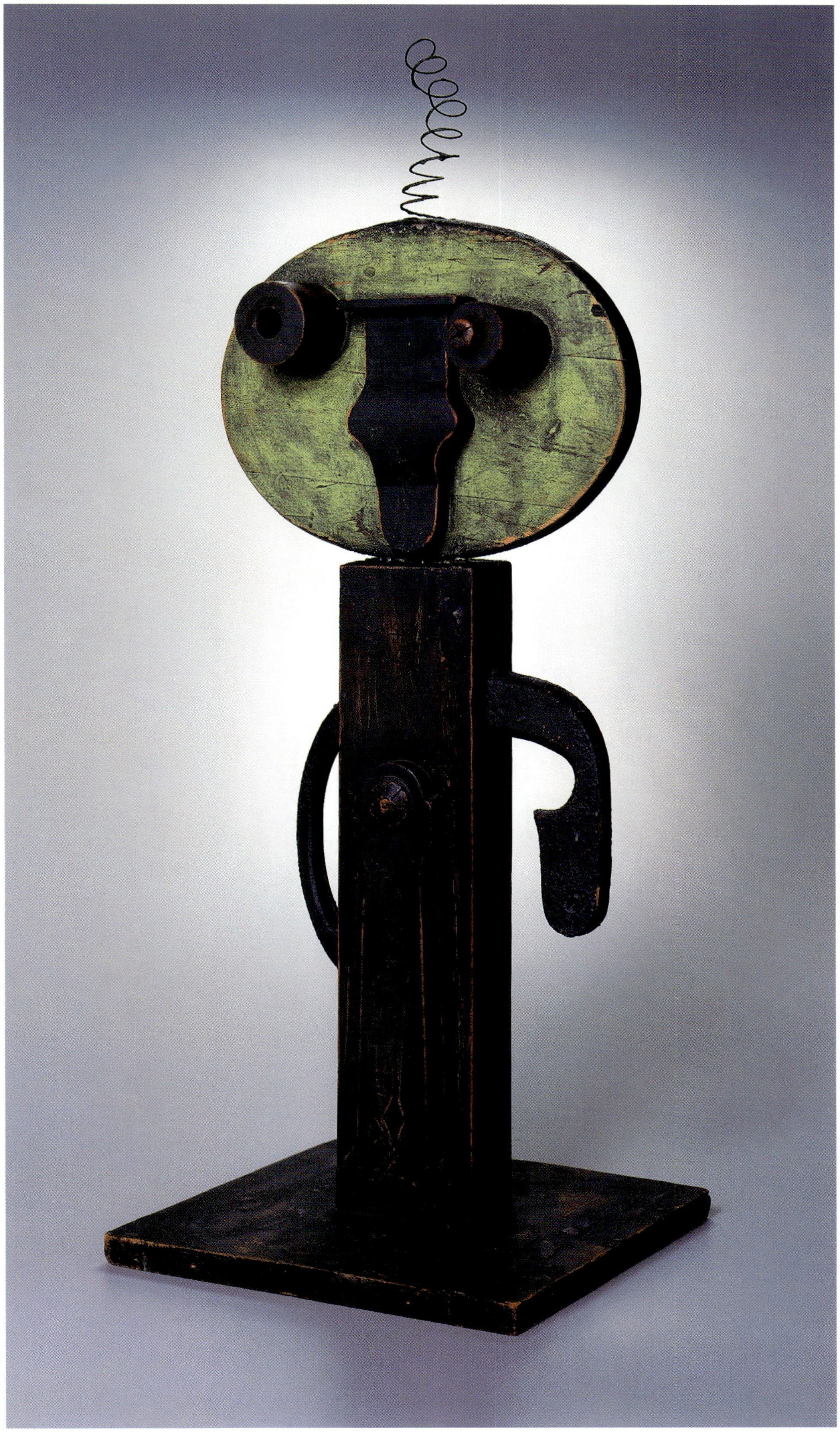

VOODOO, VIOLET, AND BLUE, 1965

Sometimes I start with an idea or image, but more often and usually more successfully I begin by collecting colors, textures, shapes; manipulating and playing with them until a structure starts. Then the work begins to have a character of its own, to demand things; and I must listen. If communication goes wrong, I stop, destroy, and change. Destruction and change are vital to creation. The element of change is important to my work. It makes for surprises and the unexpected is exciting.

William Halsey, 1995[26]

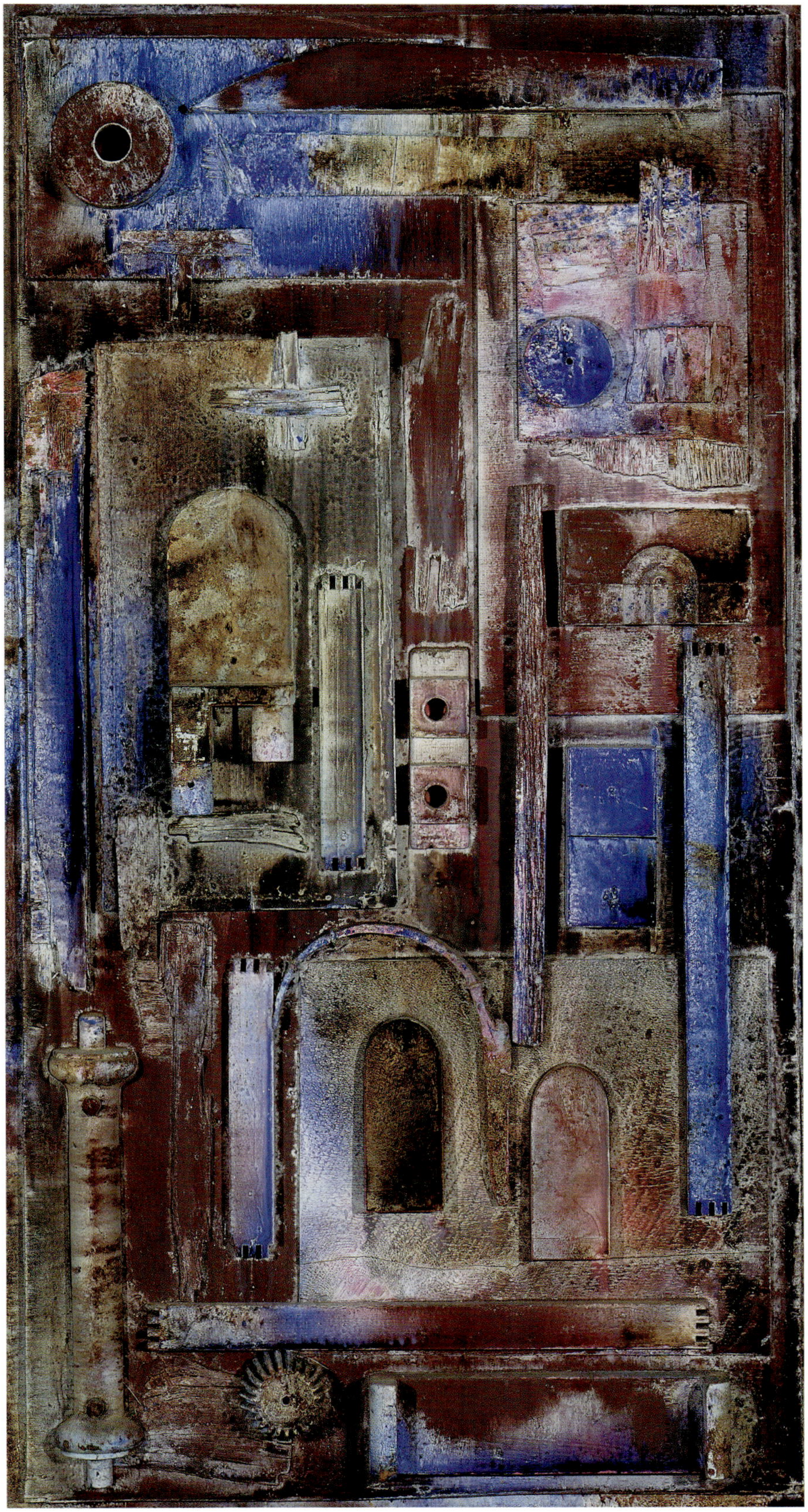

White Counterpoint, 1966

His work, even when obviously experimental, has always shown great sureness, a decidedly masculine strength and an intellectual approach to linear design which is ideally complemented by the rich subtleties of his palette. A superb colorist, he engages one's emotions much as does the composer whose music stirs one's soul to its depth, at the same time . . . delighting one's mind with the intricacy of his design.

anonymous author, 1958[27]

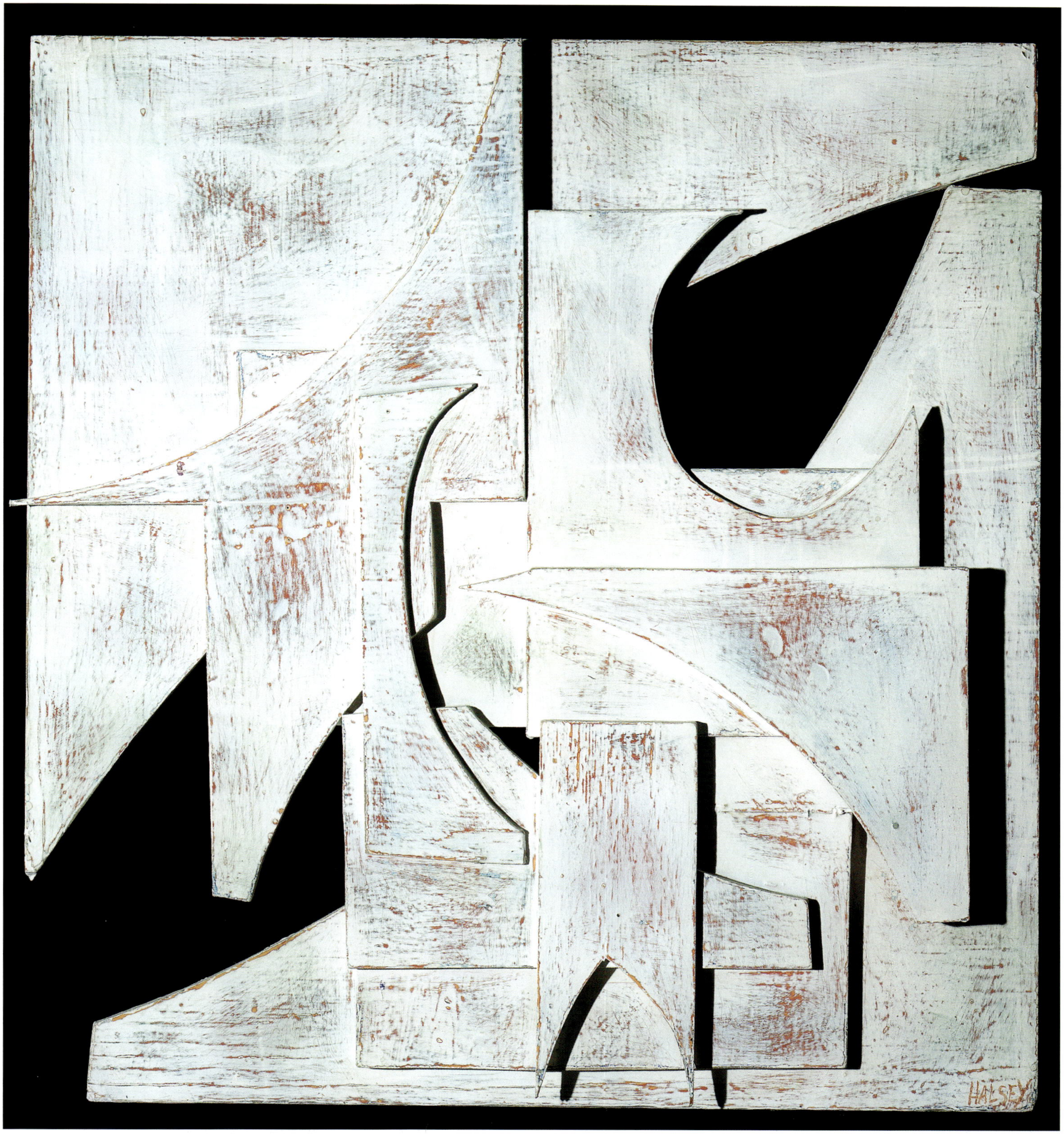
HALSEY

RED ORBIT, 1969

I used to paint subjects–street scenes, landscapes, still-life, portraits. People liked the paintings, but mostly they liked the subjects. This hurt my ego–I didn't want my work to be liked just because the subject was appealing. I wanted it to be liked because of the painting. . . .

My work now is about color, shape, movement, direction, space, rhythm, texture. Each painting, or collage, or whatever, is an object in itself, a physical thing–not a picture of a thing.

William Halsey, circa 1968[28]

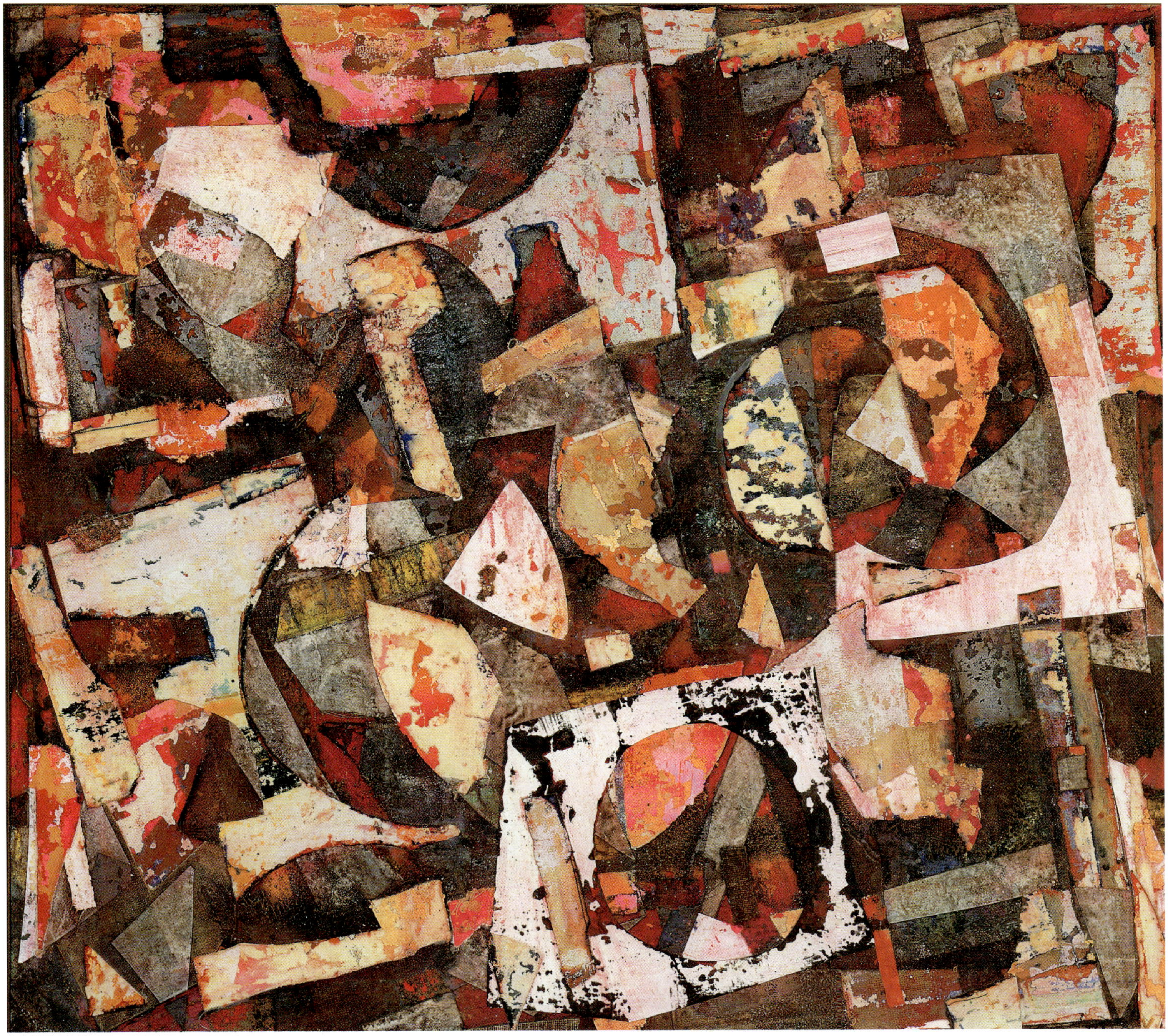

RED EARTH, YELLOW MOON, 1970

Abstraction is like an alphabet of shapes and colors and forms. Some recur in variations: various rectangles, triangles, circles, semi-circles, and repeat themselves, like an ice skater with a repertoire he's comfortable with. I keep going back to the layers of color underneath and the linear patterns. Colors that represent emotions. I use a lot of red, purple–hot, but also tropical blue. Color by itself does not do enough.

William Halsey, 1998[29]

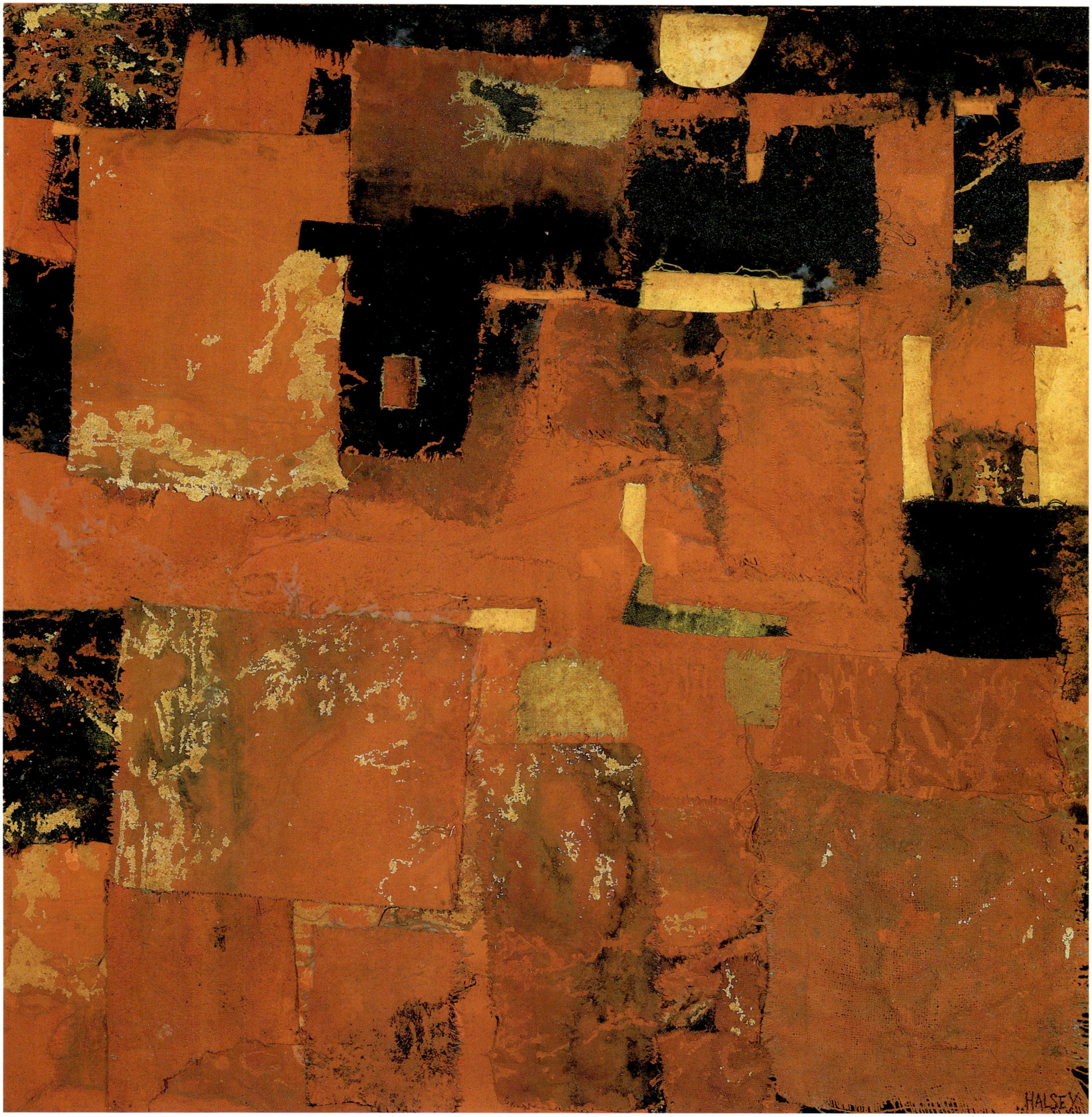
HALSEY

Sea Monument, 1966

What to me is most interesting in the psychology and special sensitivity of William Halsey is the combination of his root feelings with a universal form of expression. He has absorbed the esthetics of his own territory, the special tones and forms of Charleston and the Low Country. Yet none of this led to a provincialism in view, a passion for the familiar. His concern has been for form and color, in abstract or representational expressions, wherever inspiration is to be found.

Robert Marks, 1977[30]

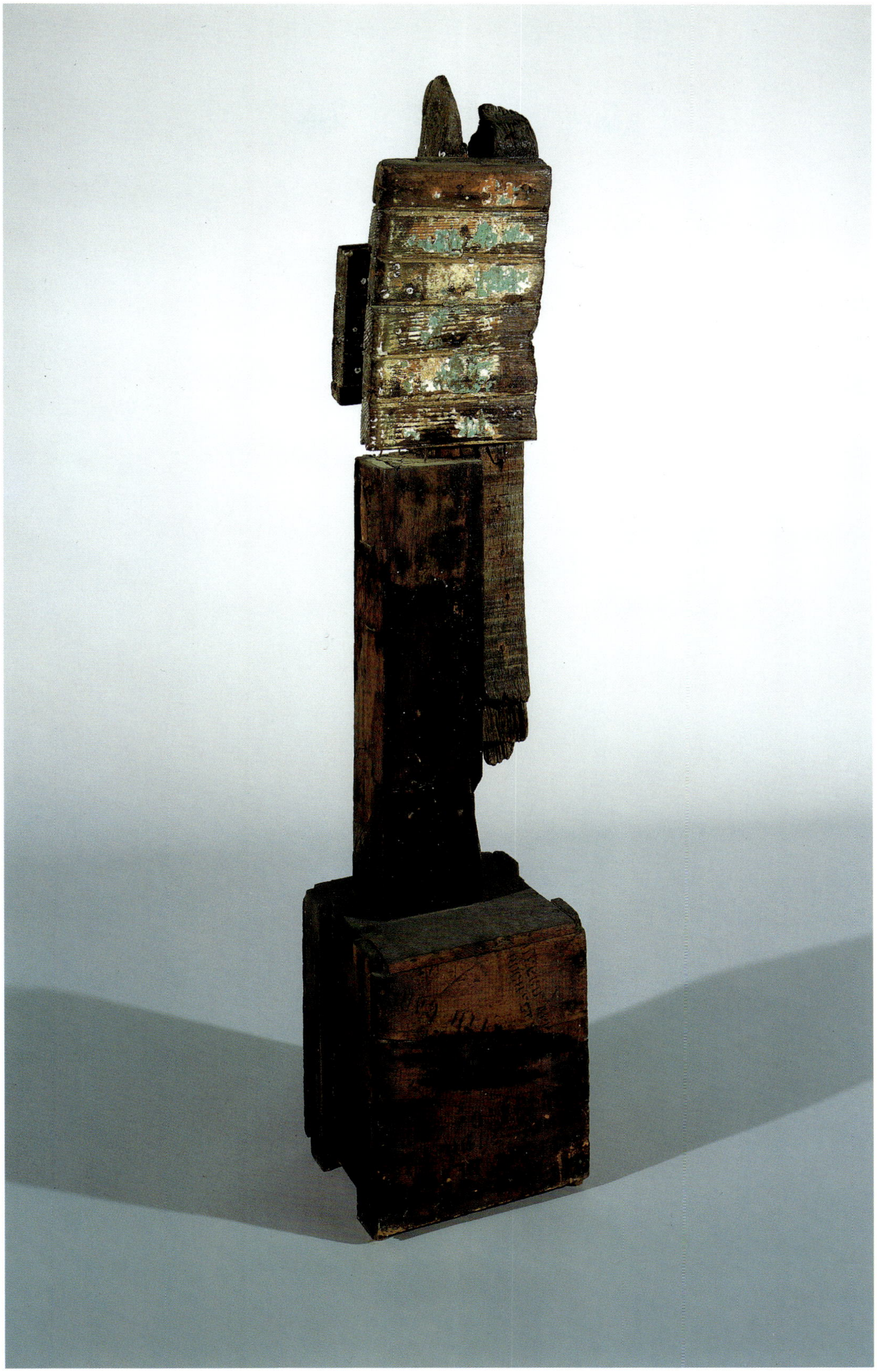

Black Chair II, 1968

What I paint is what I am. Every painting is, in one way or another, a self-portrait. Since what I am changes from day to day, and from year to year, what I paint changes, too. . . . Nowadays, it is considered very necessary to acquire a "style," meaning a technical formula for painting. Real style comes not from a technique of painting, but from a philosophy of seeing and living. Bonnard had real style because he had no style at all. His individuality was a result of vision, not of a clever brushstroke.

William Halsey, 1960[31]

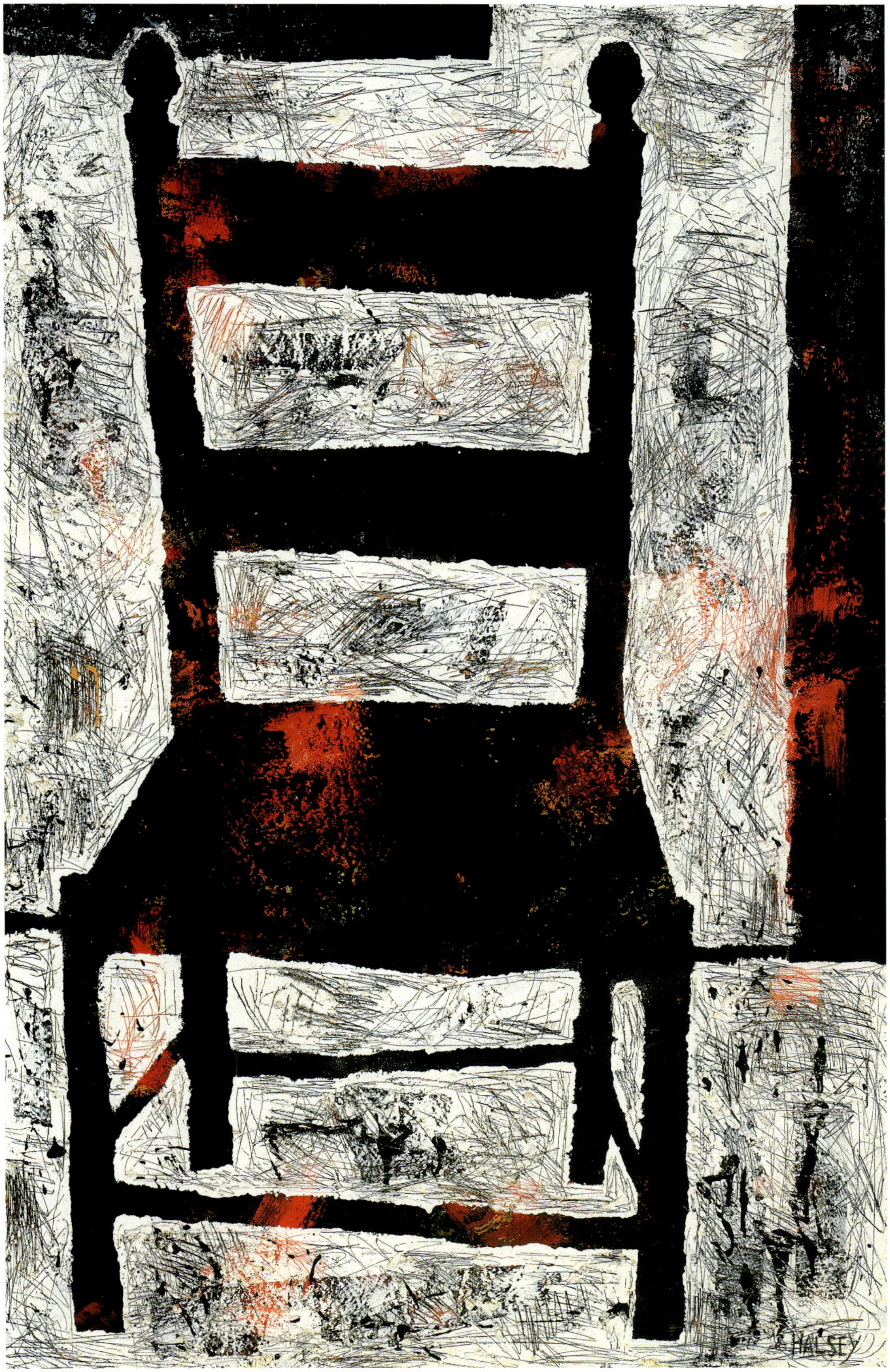
HALSEY

Old Man, 1972

The original title was *Old Man About to Disappear*–a painting I did of my father when he was quite old. He did disappear. He was ninety-two years old when he died.

Old Man is a square format. Then I tricked the space around the corner of the room, so that it's a rectangle inside a square. I put on the paint and scratched unevenly. To get texture I got marble dust in bags and mixed it in with paint to give it a grainy texture. I like surfaces like old walls, uneven surfaces, built-up surfaces, crumbling ones.

William Halsey, 1998[32]

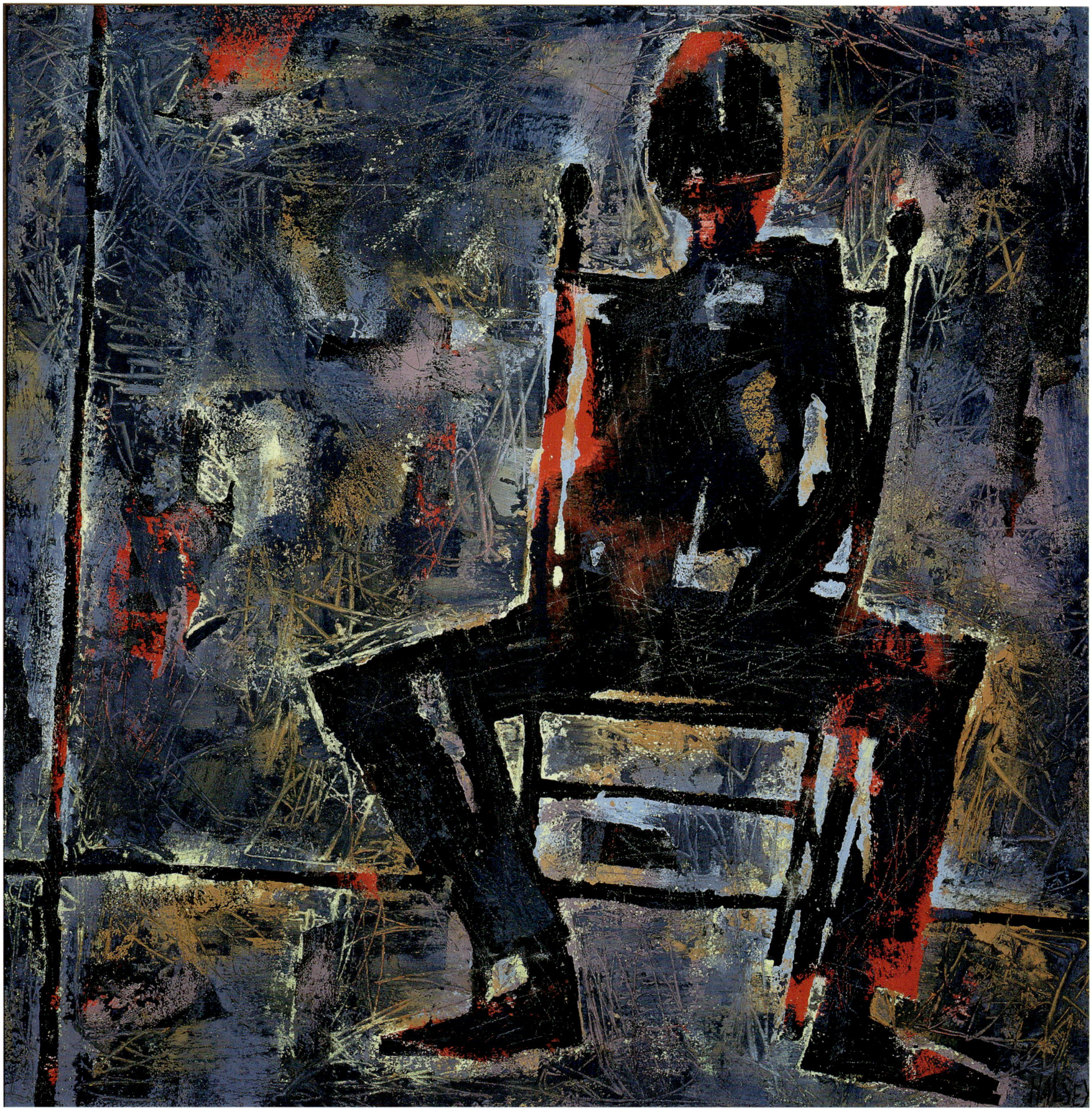

HANGED MEN, 1972/1973

Grotesque figures convey the artist's sense of being an outsider. Their shadowy silhouettes evoke a haunted introspection and isolation. The somber mood further allows the viewer to project his identity into the void created by the negative space. The primitive forms have strong affinities with the art and life of Mexico, which Halsey has visited often since studying there in 1939-1941. They were also influenced by Jean Dubuffet's *l'art brut*.

Anthony F. Janson, 1978[33]

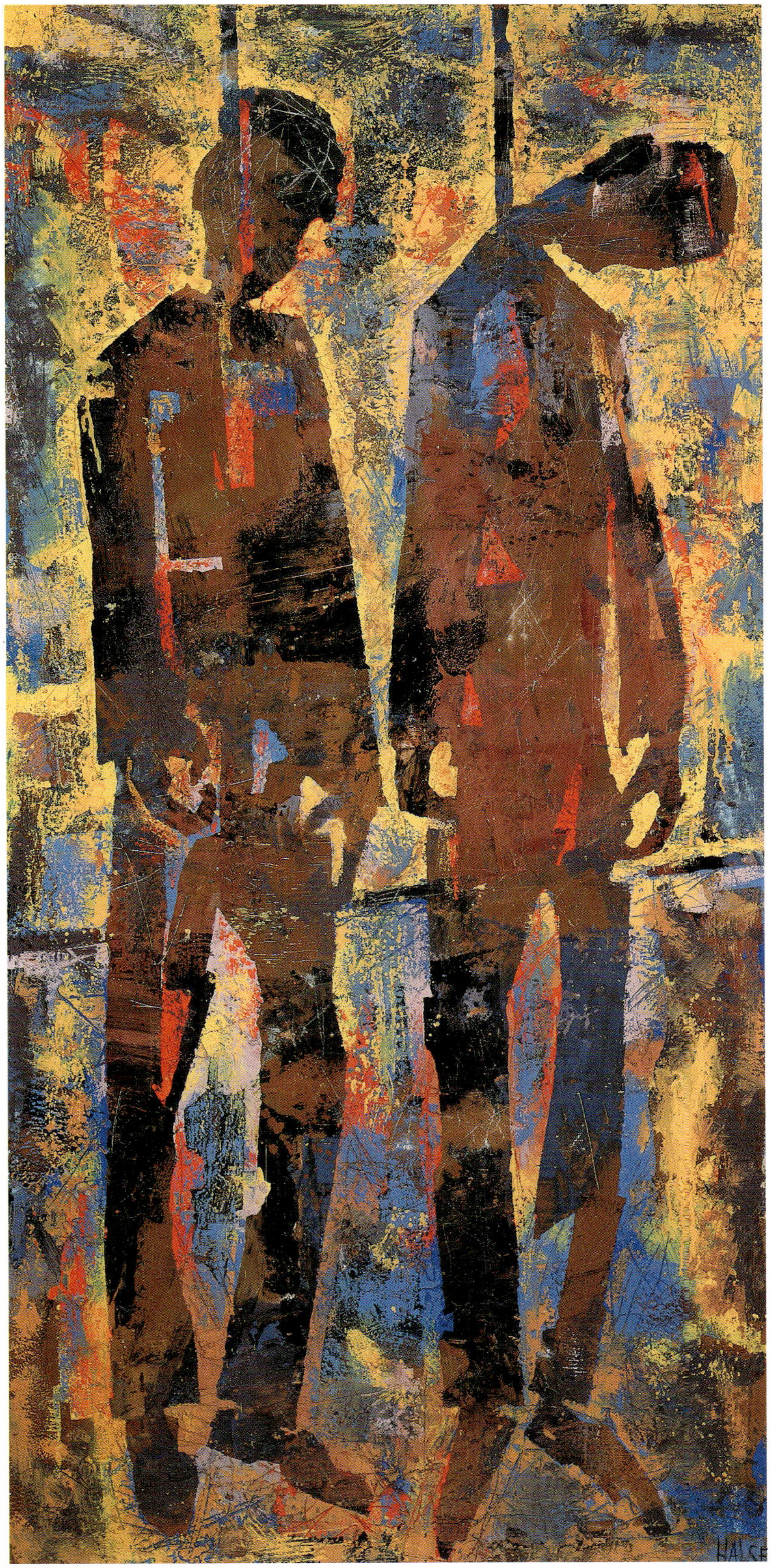

Stones of Time: Air, 1982

For many years, William Halsey has been carrying on a love affair with fragments, shards, ruins, pieces of past civilizations. This enchantment is not simply a nostalgia for things past. A large part of it is visual-physical pleasure derived from the color, the feel, the broken edges and worn surfaces, the accidents produced by time and weather. The enigmatic quality of things not quite complete, the mystery of forms and symbols not quite understood, adds excitement. The fact that he cannot decipher the Maya language or read Etruscan hieroglyphics does not detract from their significance for him but, rather, adds to it. "If I knew what the words said, I would simply read the message and not see the shapes and colors," Halsey says.

anonymous author, 1982[34]

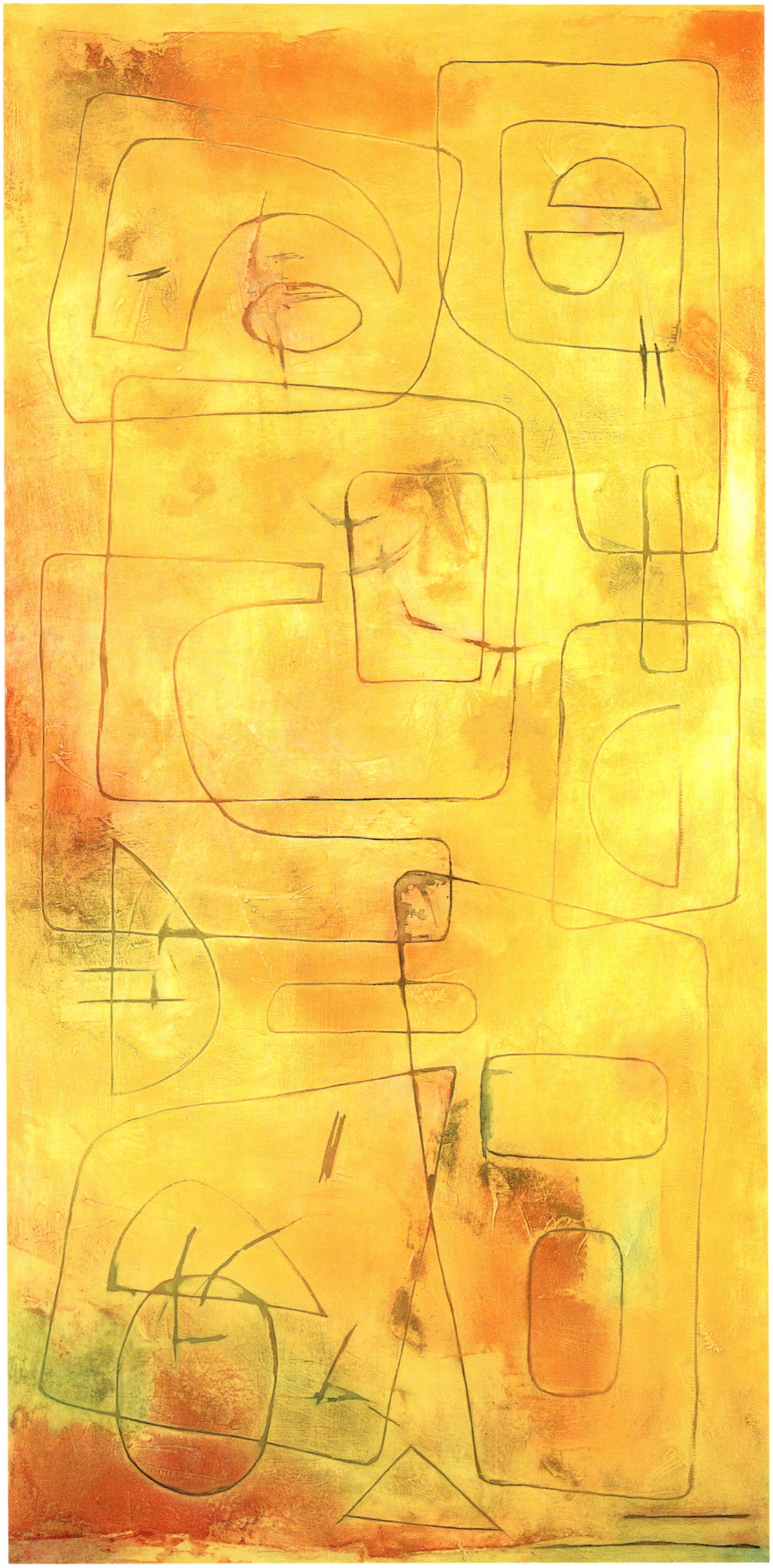

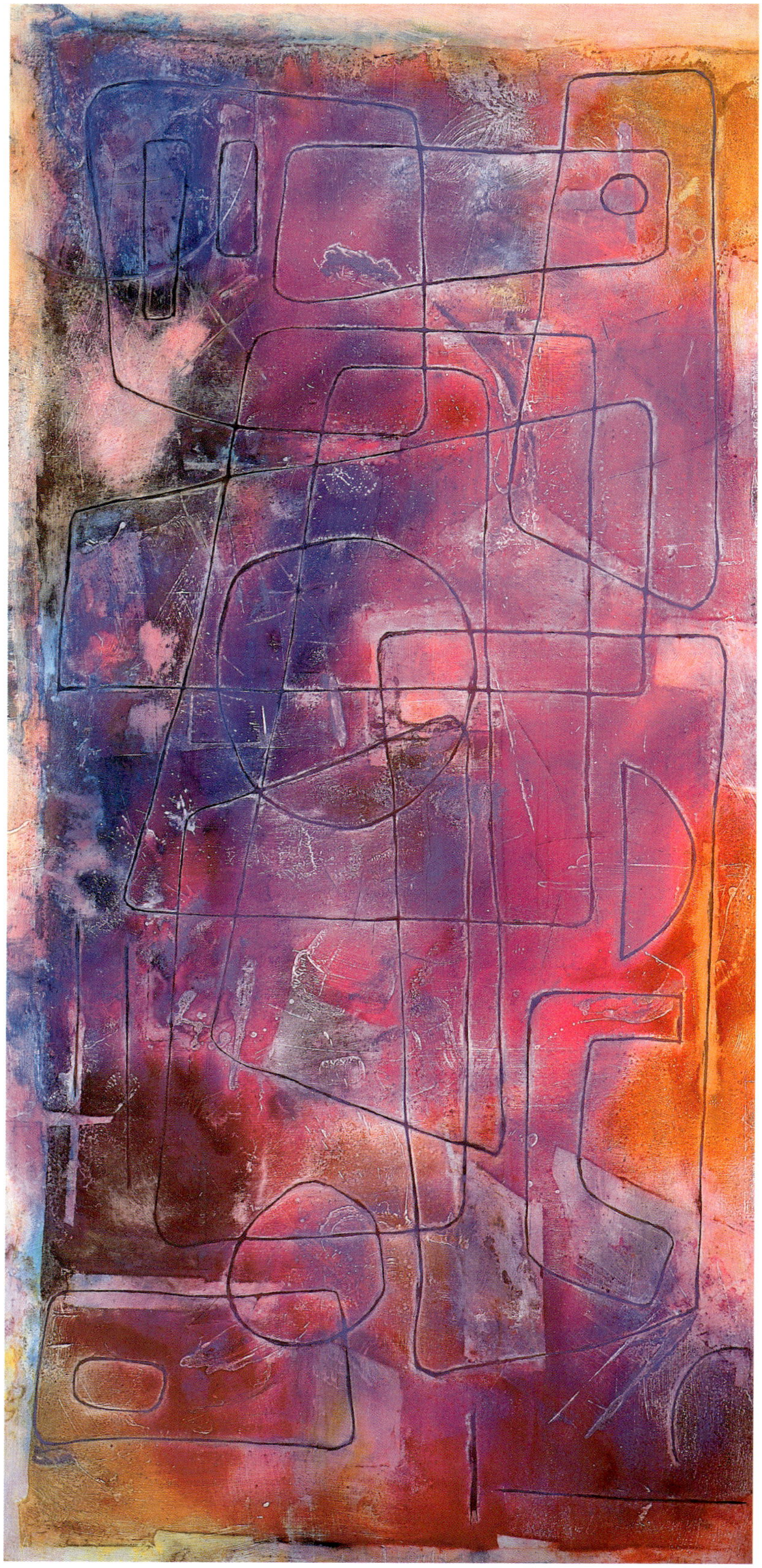

Stones of Time: Itzmina, 1982

Stones of Time: Fire, 1982

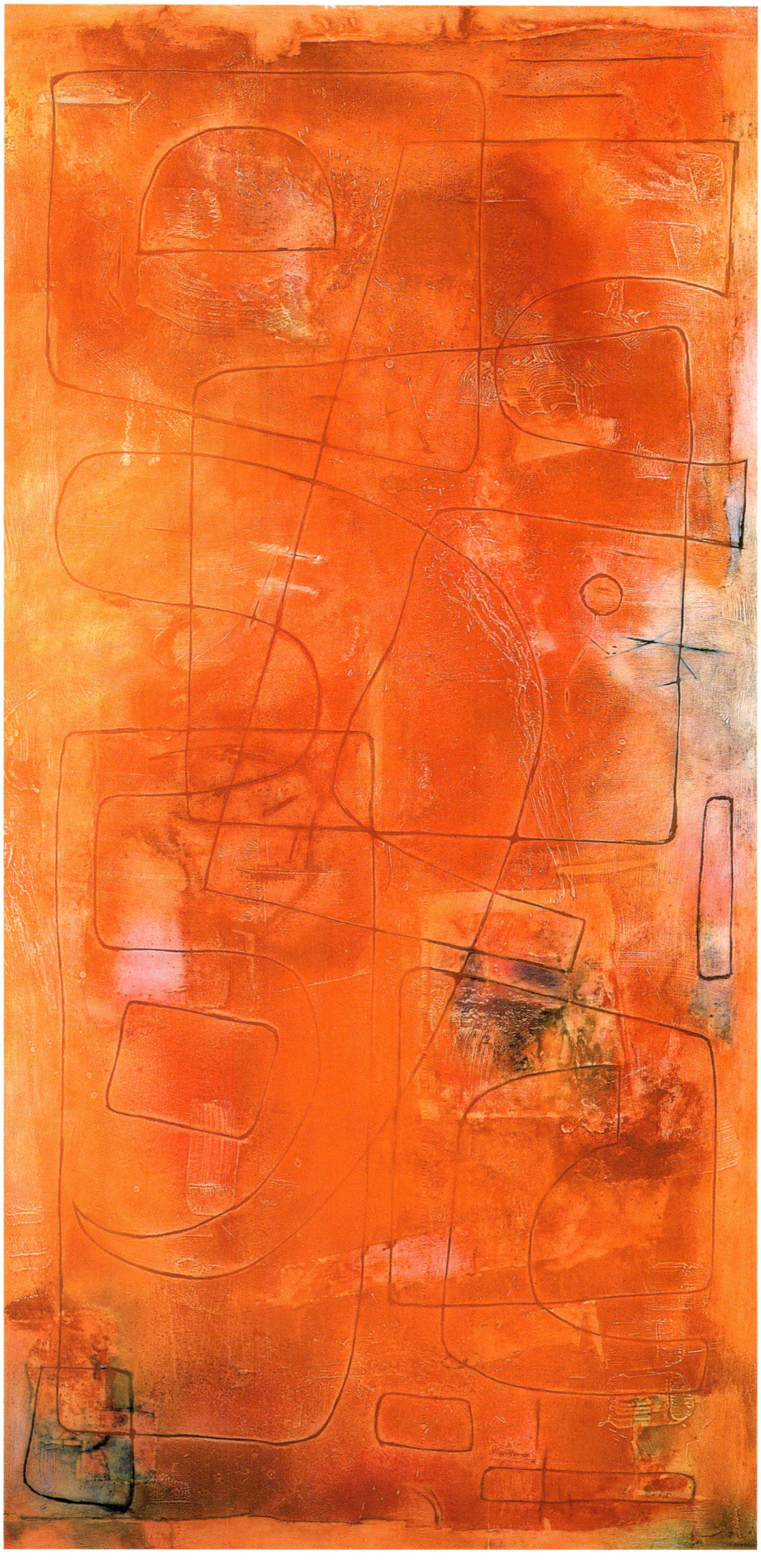

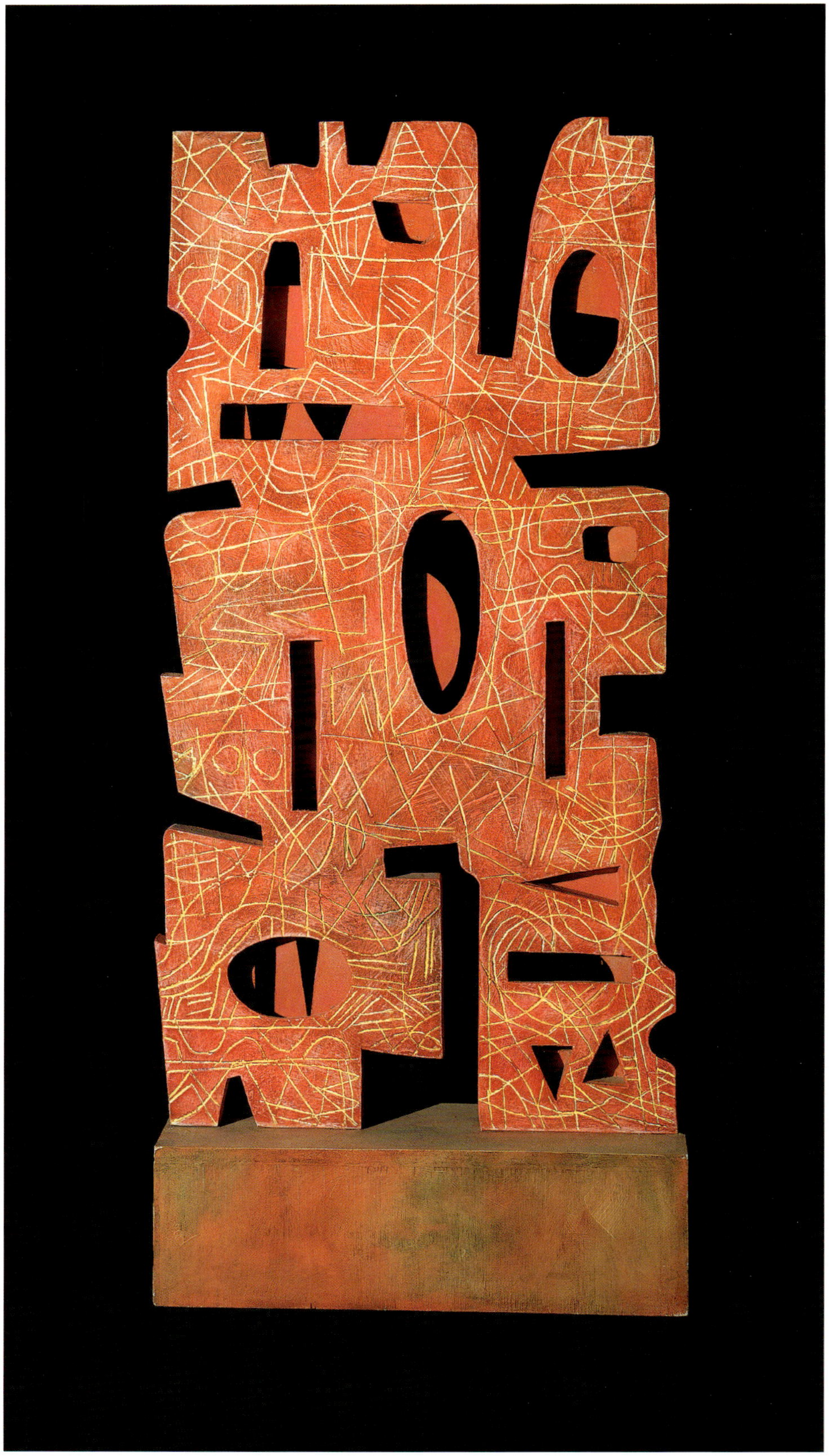

Two-faced Graffiti God #1, 1985

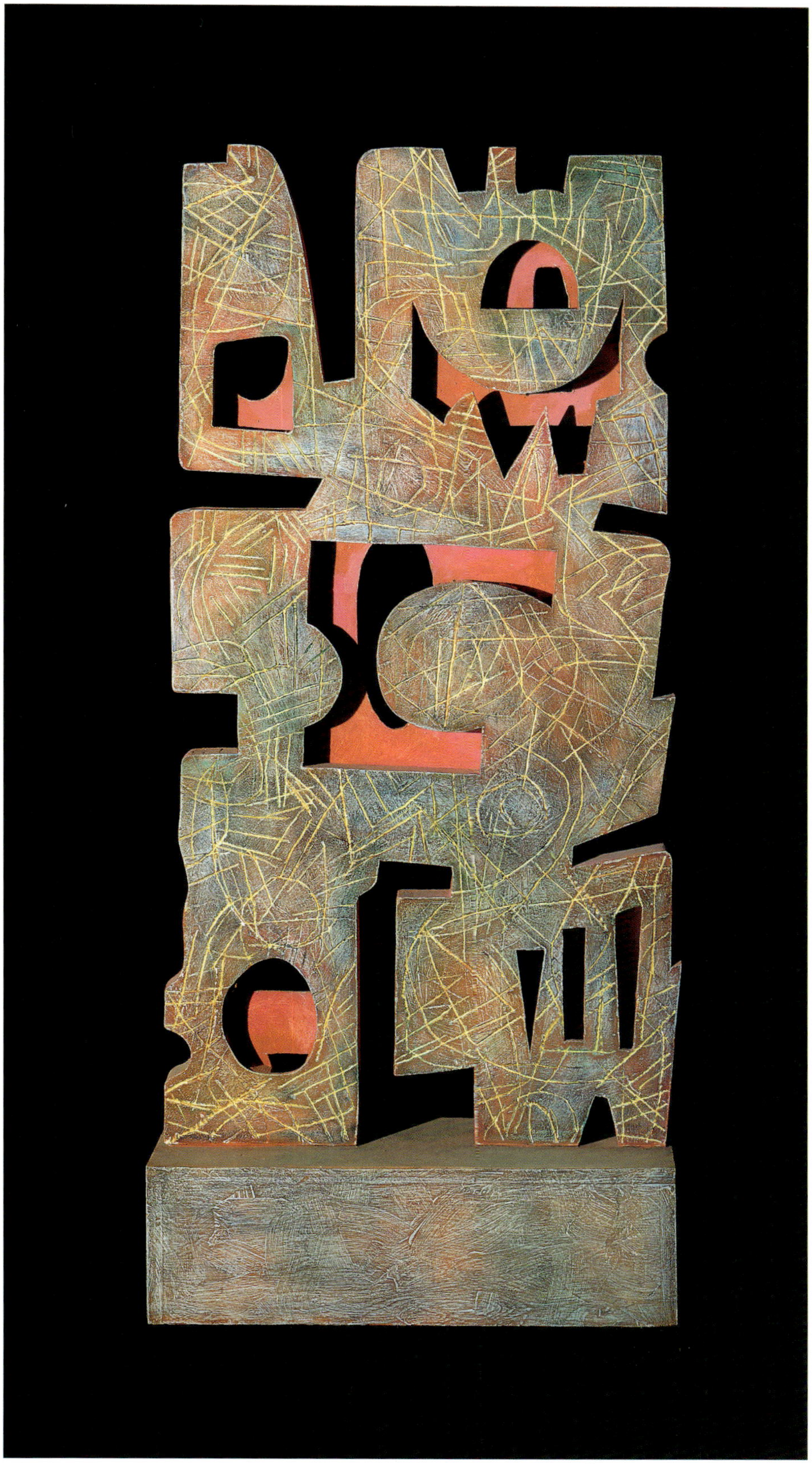

Double Congo Doors, 1986

The collages and paintings are, in a sense, a story of environments and involvements. I grew up in an impoverished Charleston, enchanted with colors of flaking plaster, old tiles, brick walls, cobbles, and rotting wood. I lived in Mexico, and since then have carried on for half a life a love affair with Mayan ruins and stone stelae. The textiles of Peru and Guatemala made imprints on my mind and work. Influences of African sculpture mix with pre-Columbian. One series of collages was started when a long-time friend, who is a dealer in African art [Merton Simpson], sent me boxes of textiles made in Zaire, patterned with designs symbolic to their makers, but to me fascinating for their abstract qualities. What I do now is, I hope, contemporary, but also related to the art of past civilizations, to a universal language of man.

William Halsey, circa 1982[35]

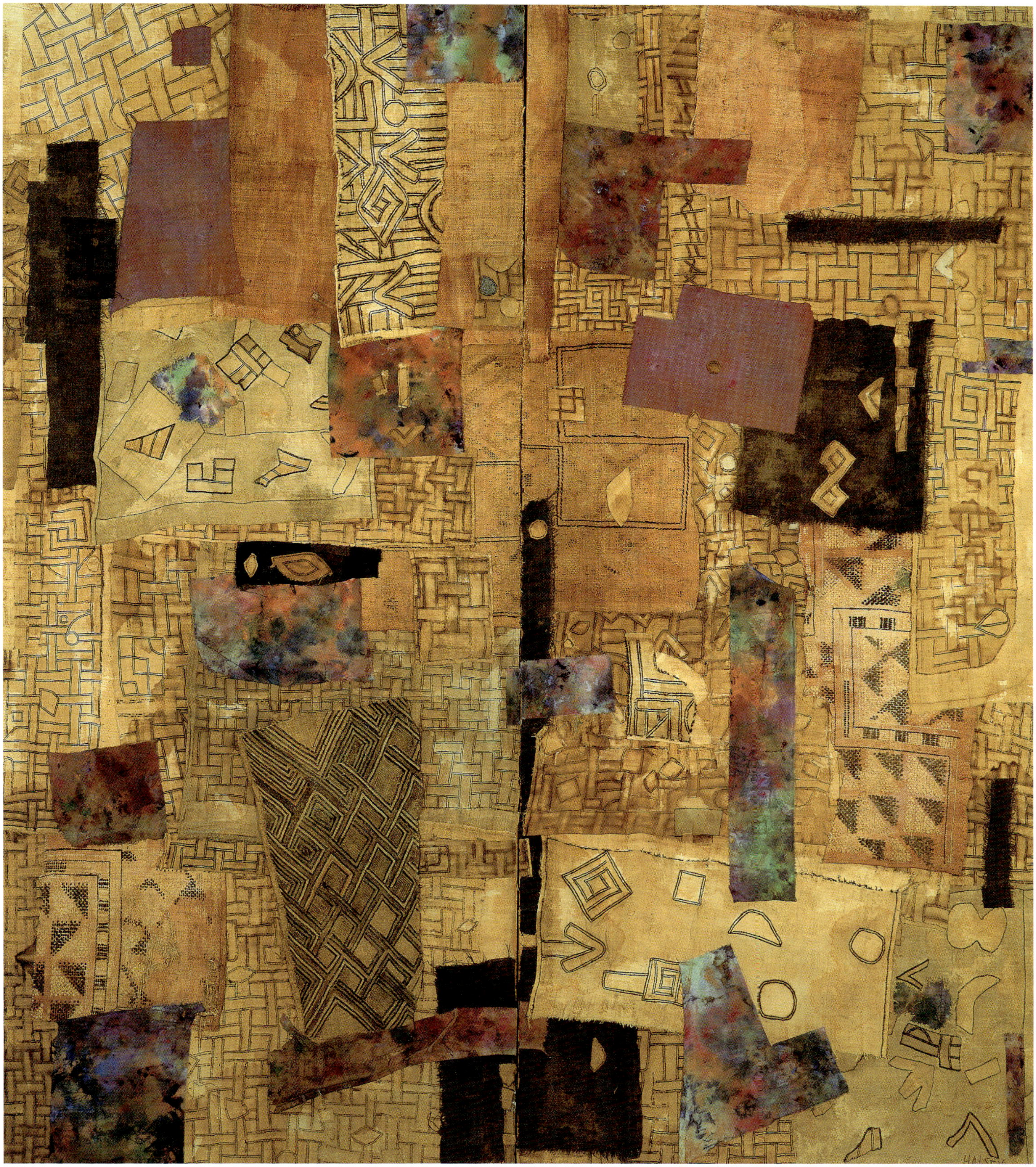

FIGURA, 1988

The collages are a combination of paint rags and African textiles, combined arbitrarily. I would glue on the boards laid on the floor; put weights on boards, then look, rip off or add. Negative/positive process. I didn't have a precise image in the beginning. Some places are sewn, worn off, ripped off or faded.

William Halsey, 1998[36]

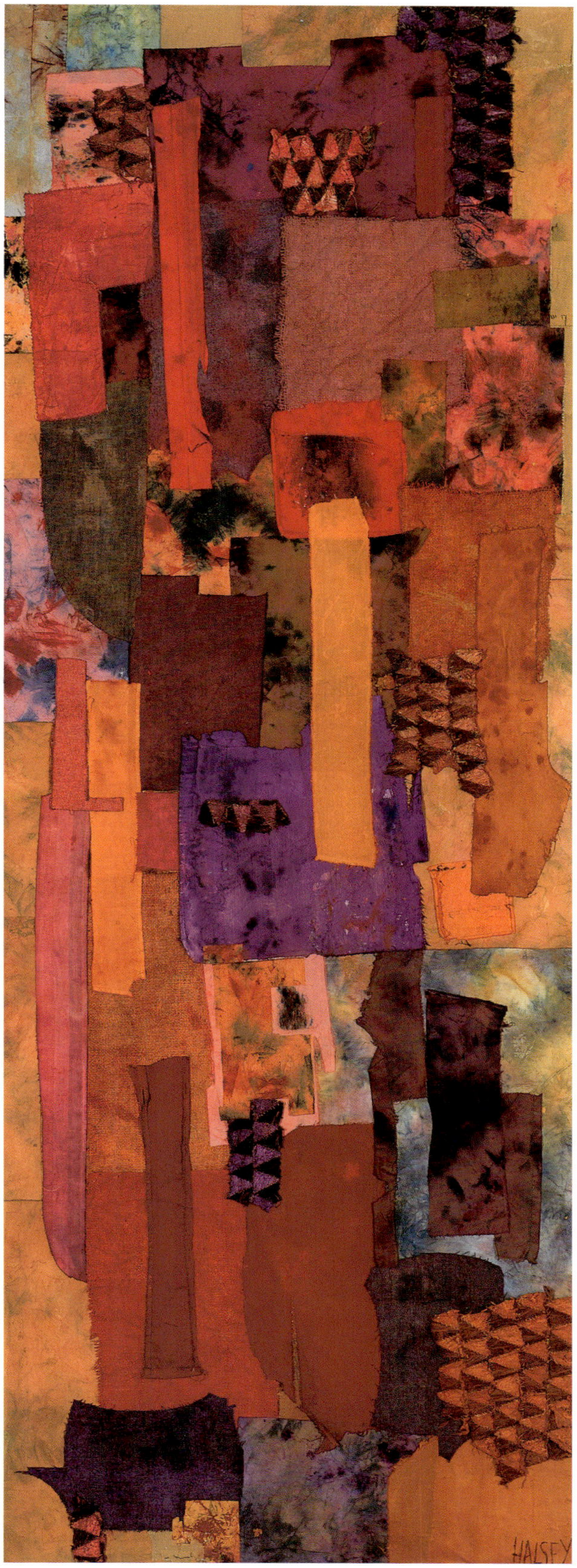
HALSEY

Moon Door, 1986

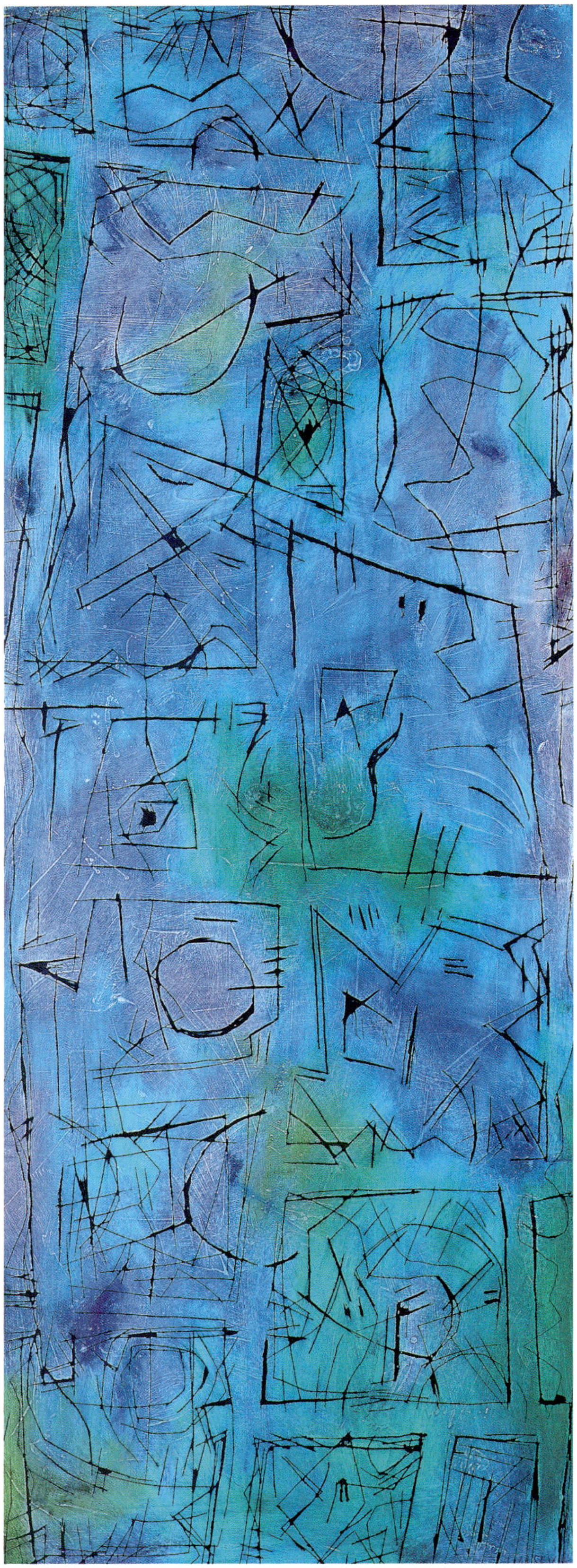

SHAMAN II, 1986

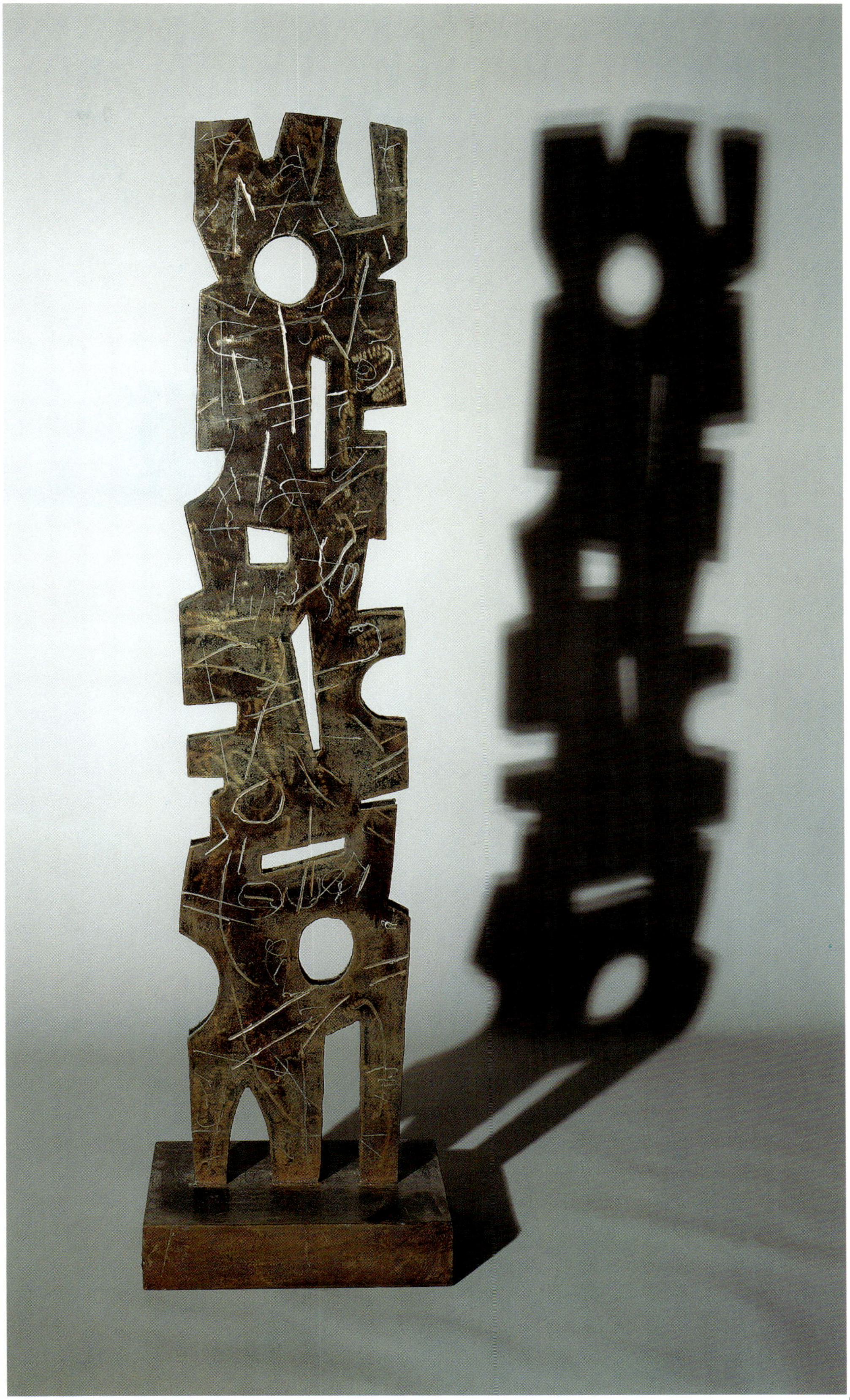

RIVER GODS, 1988

My recent paintings have to do with edges and spaces. With emptiness, nothingness and nowhereness. They are about quietness and loudness. They have to do with lightness and darkness.

William Halsey, 1980[37]

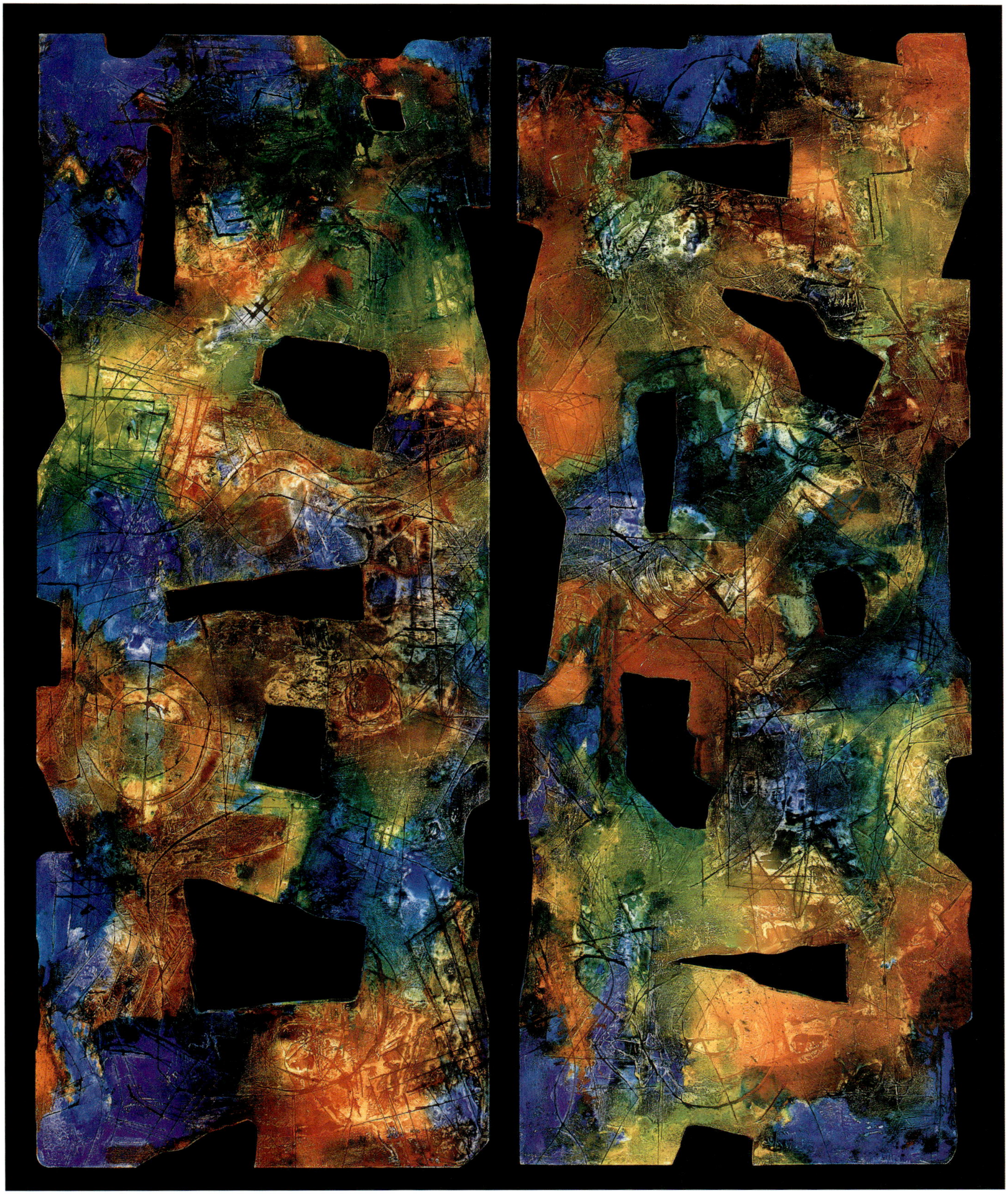

Nail, Spike, and Copper Tube, 1987

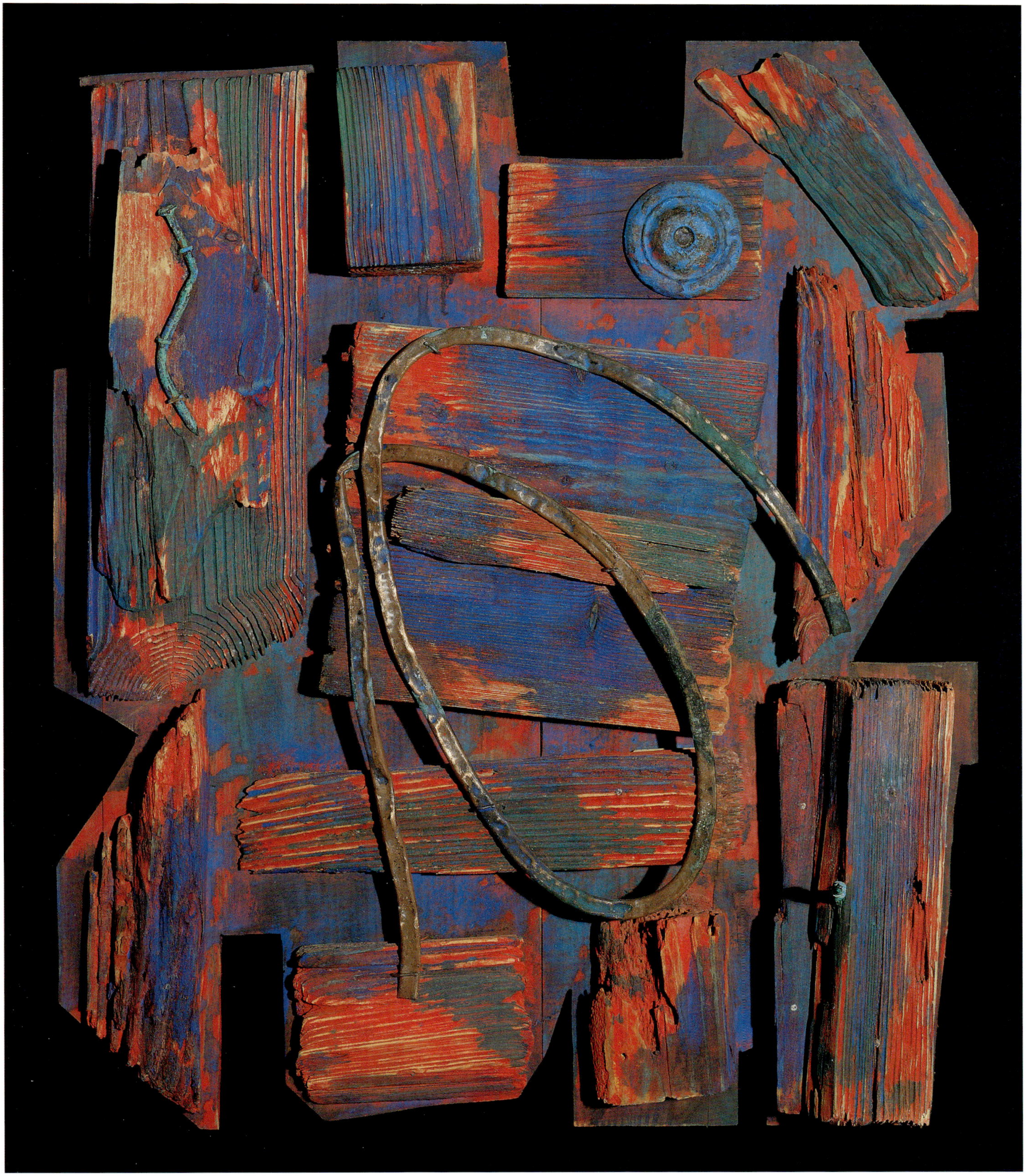

SHAMAN, 1988

My art training was traditional, and I am glad it was. I am convinced that the best modern painters are those with traditional backgrounds. Before you can depart from anything, you must know what you are departing from.

William Halsey, 1960[38]

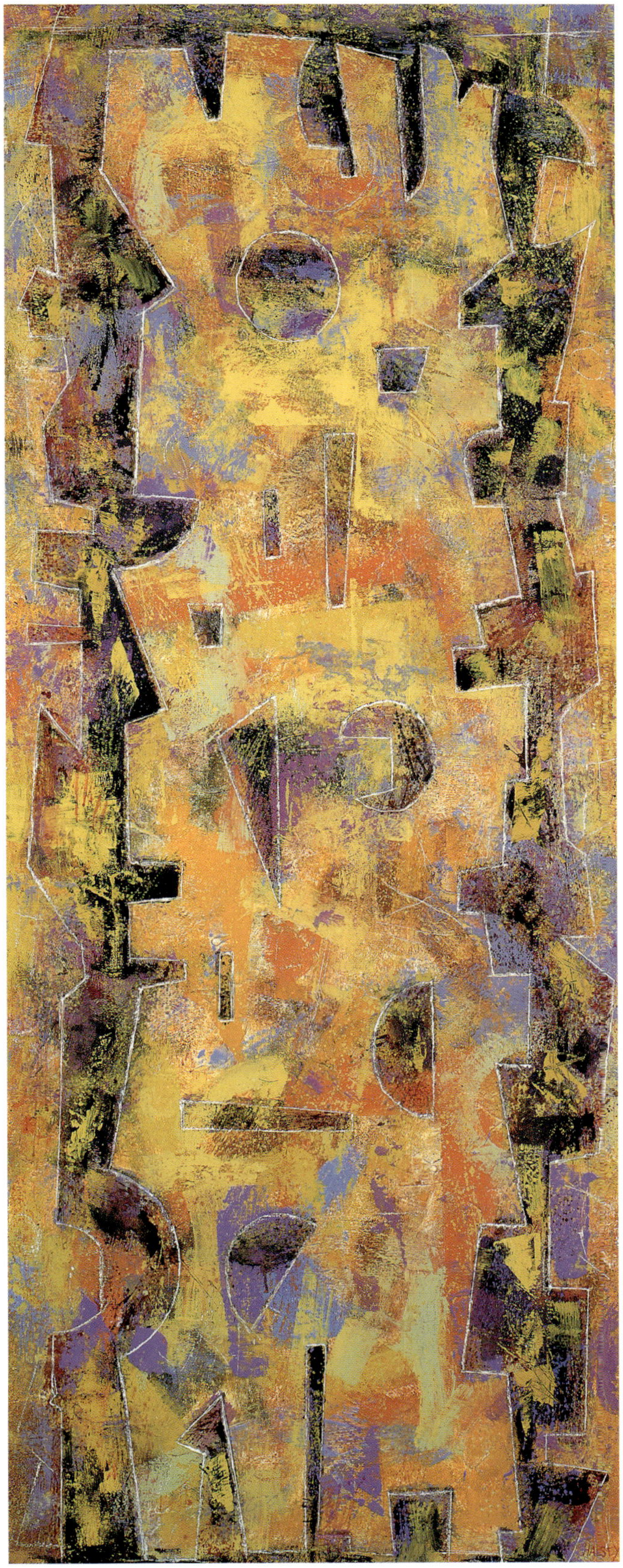

TOTEMIC, 1989

So many people go into a gallery and view an abstract painting with the question: 'What does it represent?' Some day I'd like to see the painting respond: 'What do *you* represent?' We could take the question even further and ask: 'What does a butterfly represent?' or even, 'What does a sunset represent?' Beauty should be accepted for what it is and shouldn't be analyzed for deeper meanings. Art isn't for everybody; just as baseball isn't for everybody. Those that enjoy art, enjoy it for what it is and those who don't enjoy it won't find enjoyment through attempts to see 'representation' in it.

William Halsey, 1968[39]

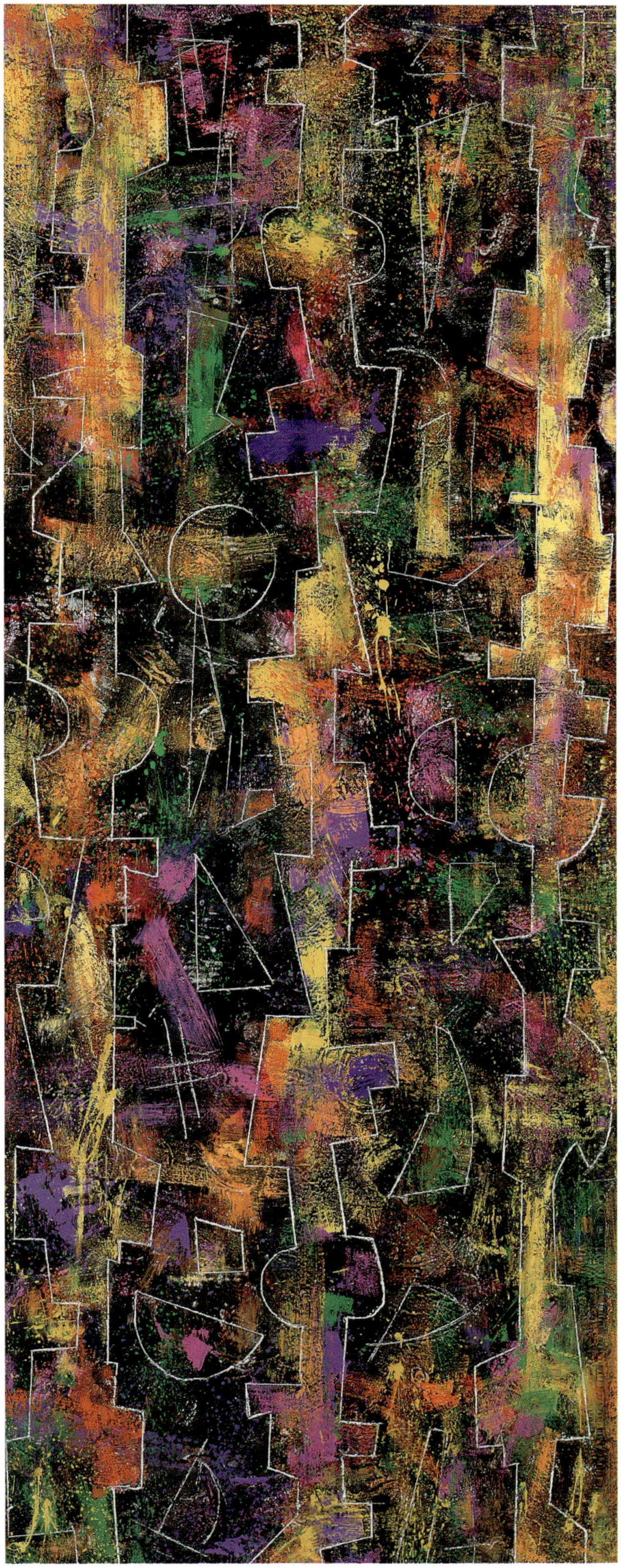

TANTARA, 1991

The restless energy and spirit of discovery which is evident in Halsey's work also carries with it the freight of the artist's attitude toward creativity. In his art there is a yoking of oppositional forces; delicacy with recklessness, the intellectual with the intuitive, and order with chaos. Throughout William Halsey's various visual output there is a consistency of vision. . . . These works invite the viewer to engage in unraveling the mysteries inherent in the materials and their handling.

Mark Sloan, 1995[40]

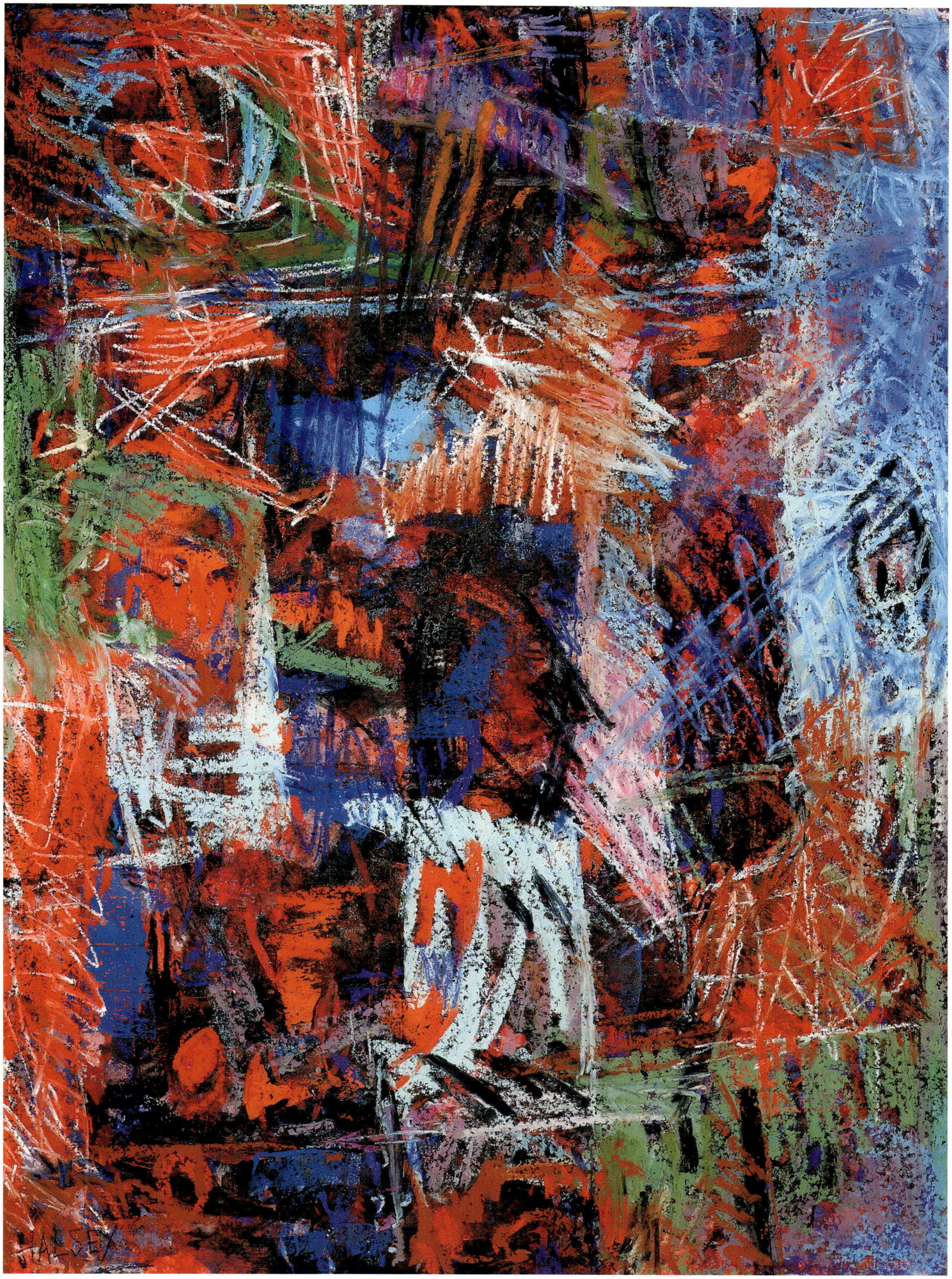

PAVANE WITH SUNLIGHT, 1993

I take a tube of paint and work on an irregular surface. I have an abhorrence of brushes. I like layers–colors underneath. I don't like things too regular. Tubes of oil-sticks–like mosaics or jewels set in. There's no subject, no center of interest: no head, no figure. Allover space and color space–an arrangement like stained glass. I like oil-sticks on paper; I can revisit them in a day. I frequently go back and work things out.

William Halsey, 1998[41]

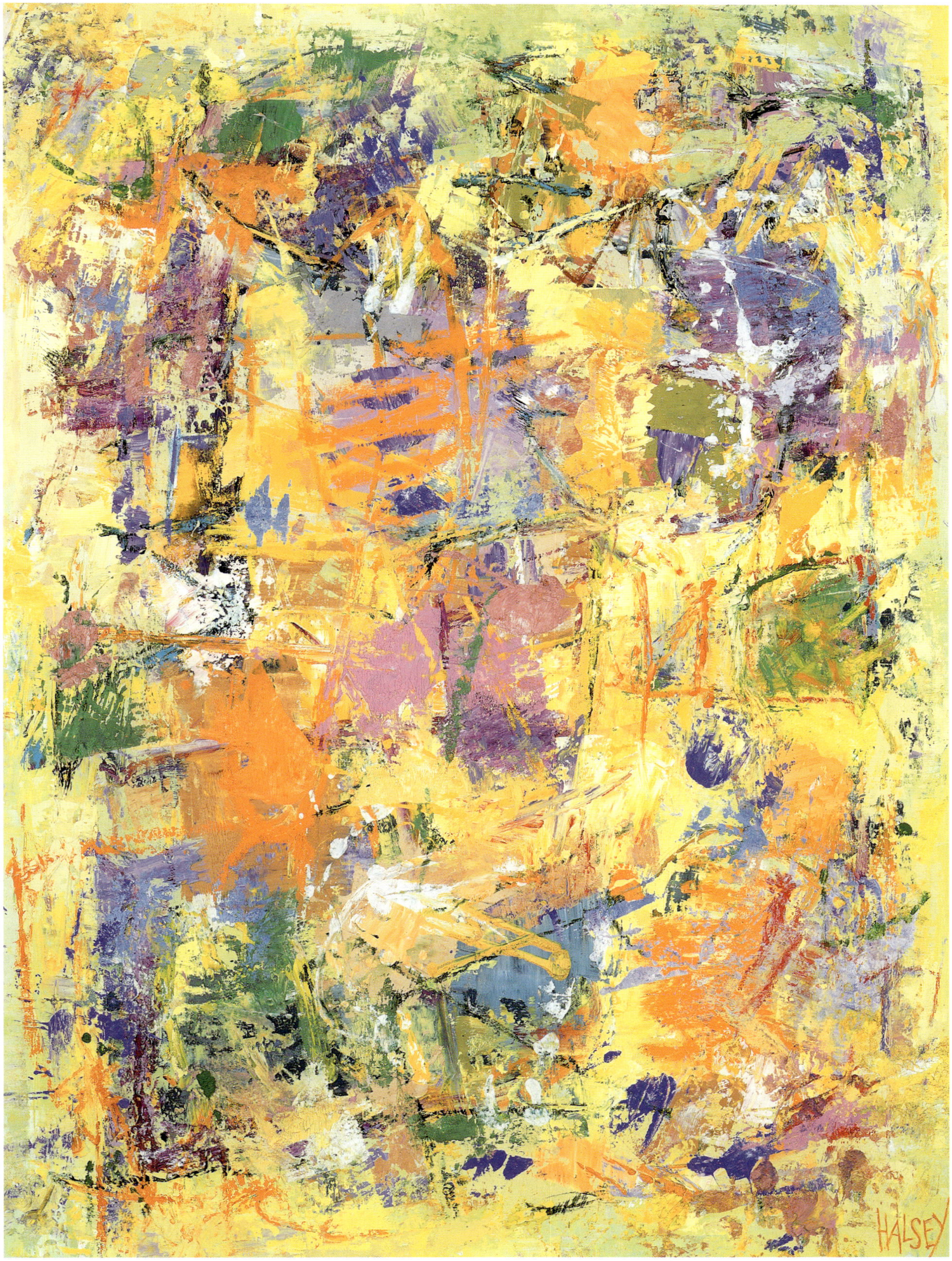
HALSEY

MAGIC CARPET, 1994

Through his paintings, collages and sculptures, as well as his untold students, Halsey has radiated a passion for expressionistic art that has seemed missionary in its commitment. . . . Halsey not only persisted in evolving his modernist sensibilities deep into another artistic era–the postmodern–but has also melded a number of this century's most intriguing stylistic inventions into an art that is distinctive and referential.

Nicholas Drake, 1995[42]

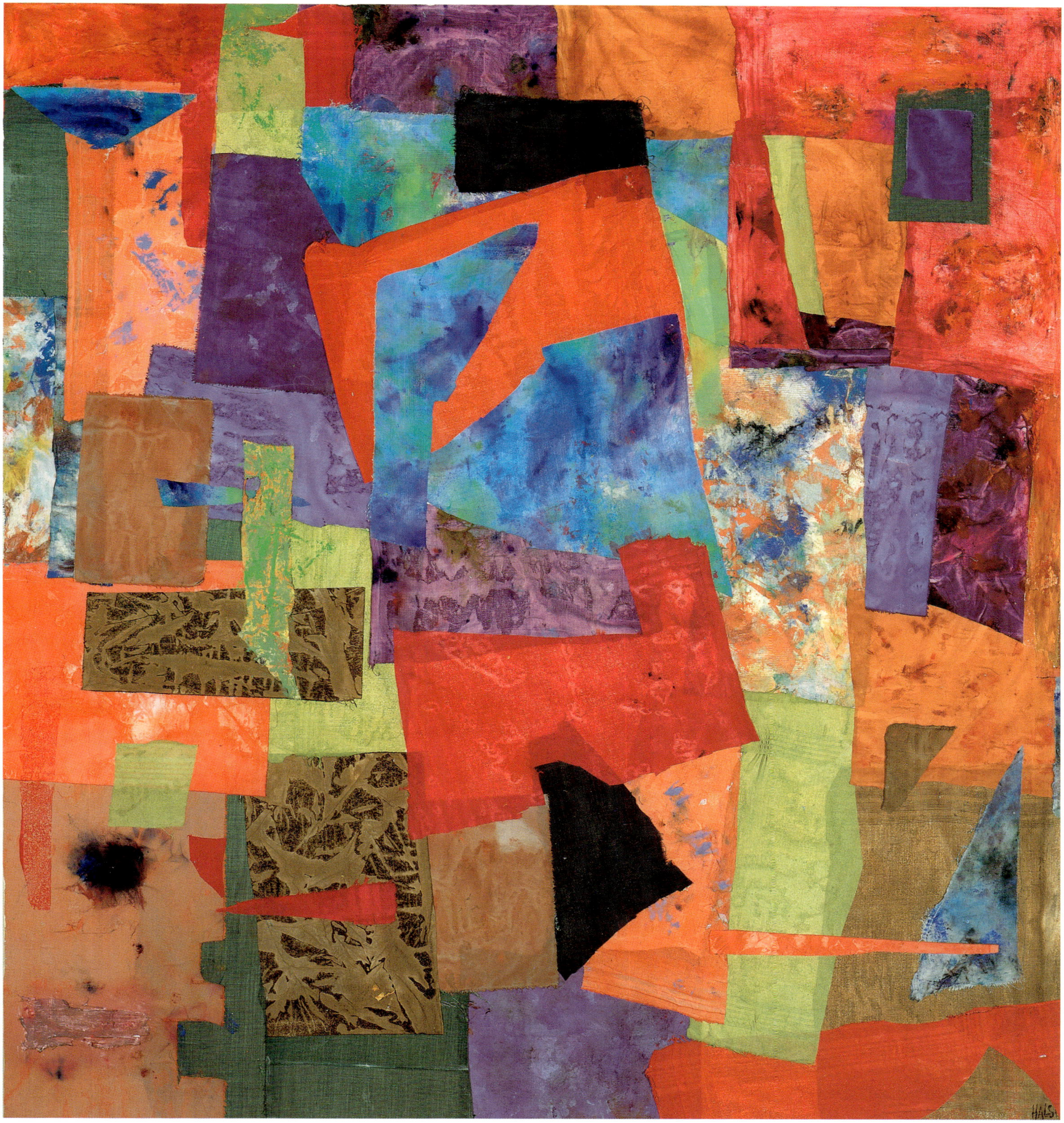

Denim, 1995

Most of my work has started with an involvement with materials–paper, cloth, paint, wood, metal, marble dust, sand; often scraps, leftovers, worn, used, and neglected. I particularly like things that have a past: torn fragments of rejected paintings, old clothes, paint rags, burlap, textiles with faded patterns, the detritus of civilization; trash that when cherished can turn into something else. I think I am an idealist, even a romantic, but I could be called a materialist because the materials I work with are so important to me.

William Halsey, circa 1982[43]

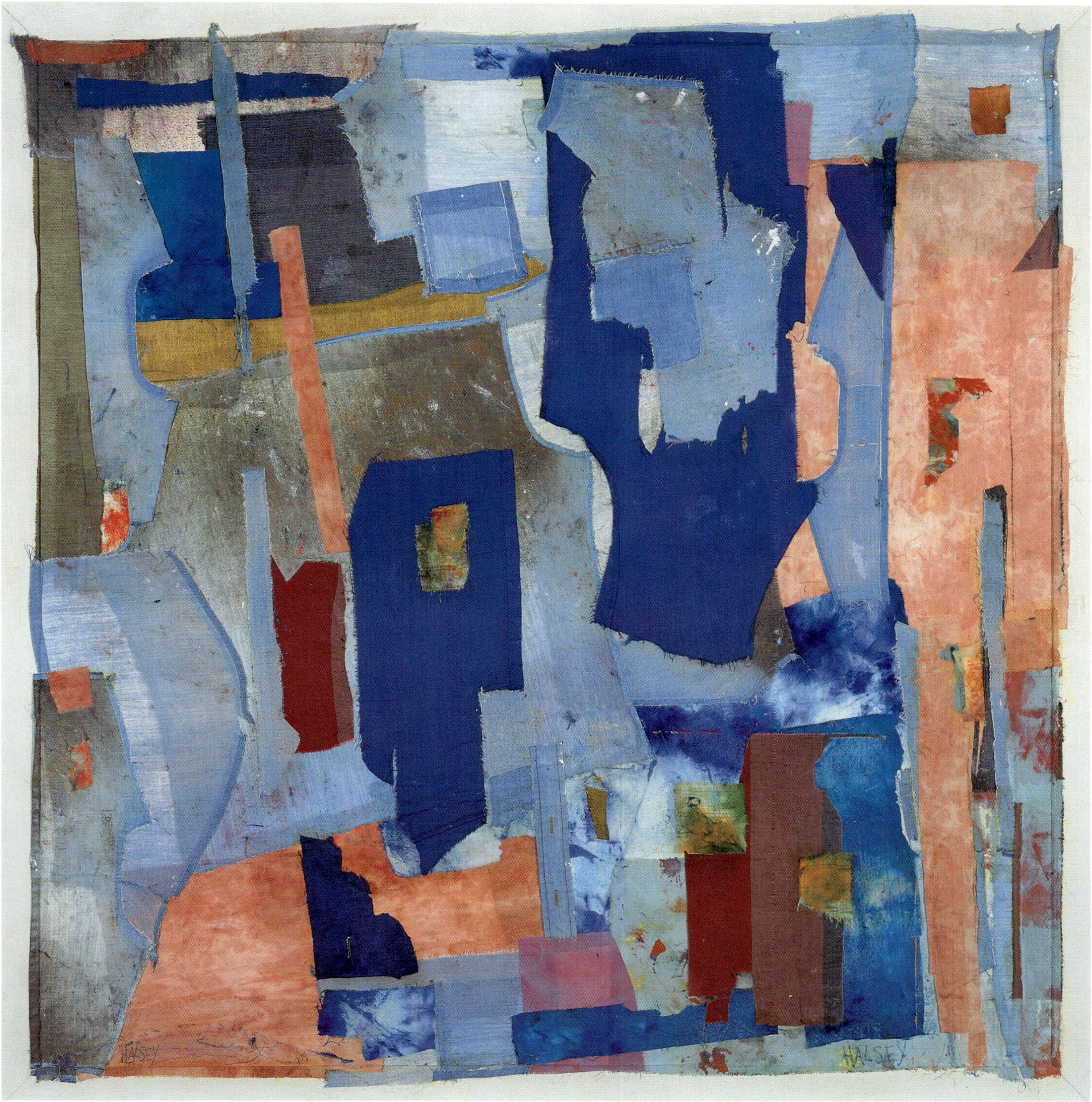
HALSEY
HALSEY

ORBIT, 1996

To make a statement about painting implies that a painting is not a statement. In the world of today, the act of painting and of being a painter is in itself a major statement. A statement of hope and an act of faith. It is also a pleasure, a pain, an exercise in futility, an adventure, and a helluva lot of fun.

William Halsey, 1994[44]

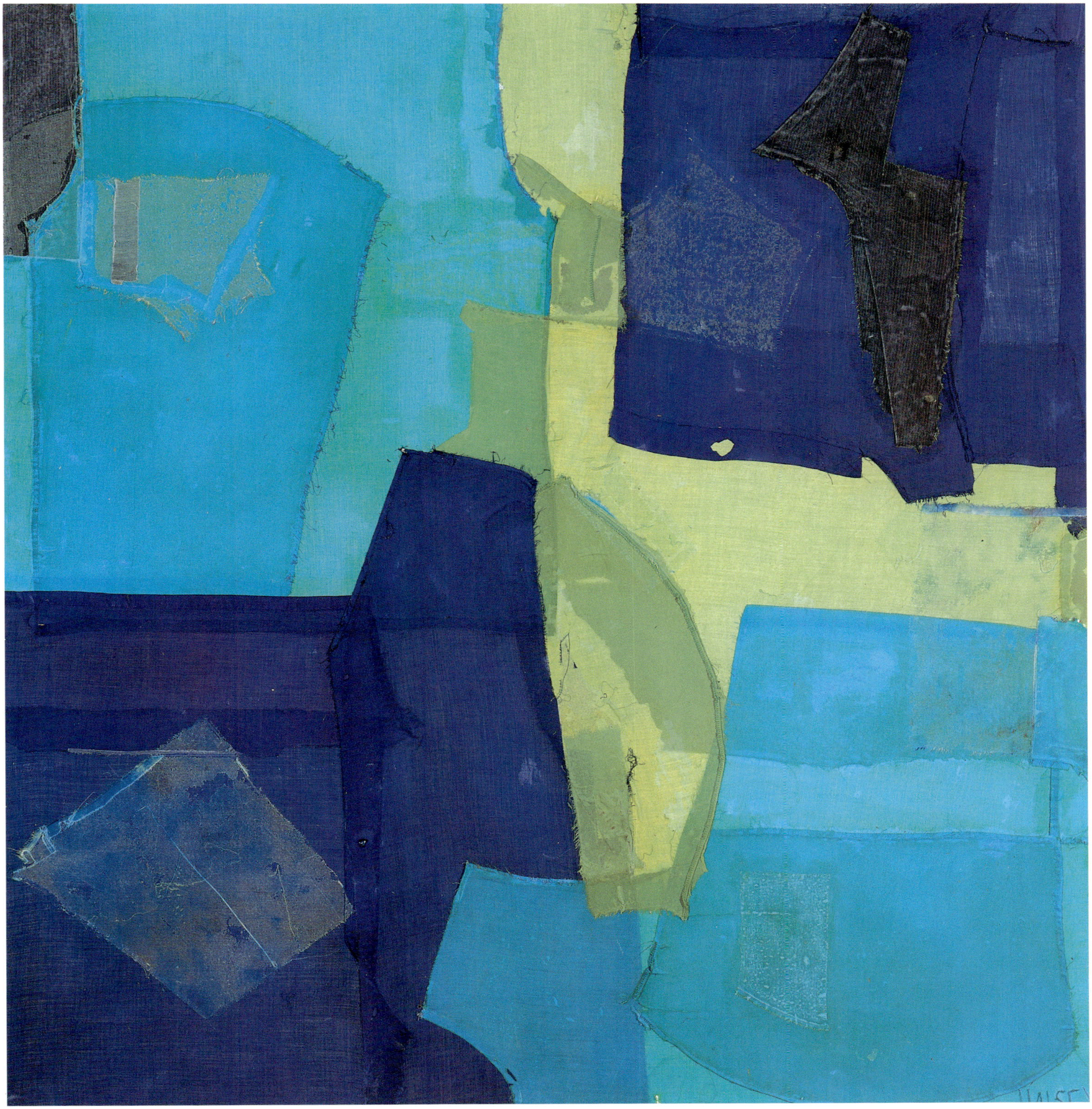

Red Square, 1997

I believe in ambiguity. Life is full of ambiguity. A painting should be open to various interpretations. Paintings are not necessarily answers–sometimes they're questions.

William Halsey, 1972[45]

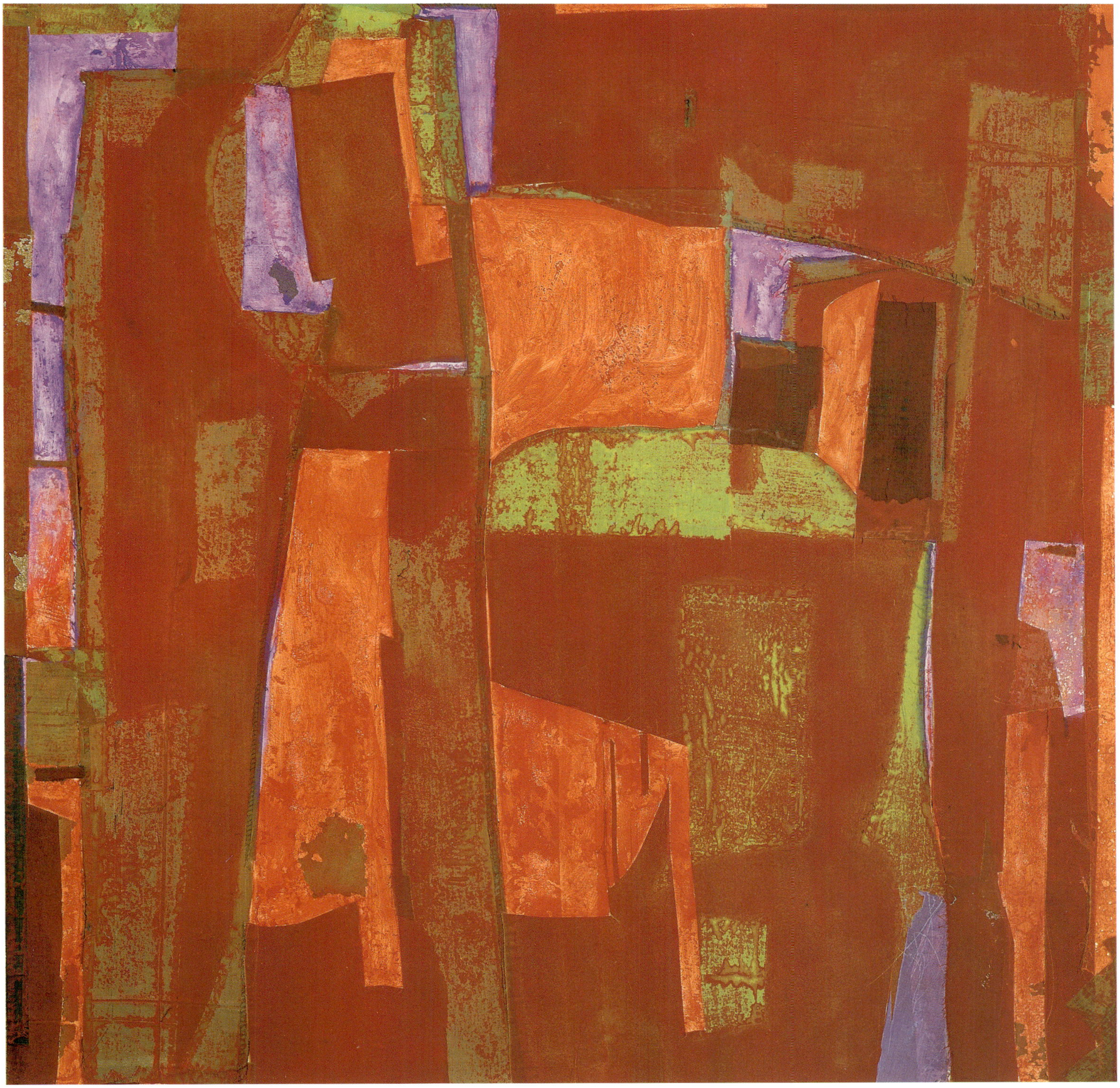

METAMORPHOSIS, 1985 / 1991/ 1998

I think I'm doing good work. I may be wrong; I may be totally wrong. But at the age I am [81], I'm not concerned about what people think. Now I do what I think is good. I'm painting directly from my internal feelings and hopefully doing what comes naturally and has some basic instinct to it. Time's getting short. You can't say, "I'm going to do what I want tomorrow."

. . . . There were times when I was terribly discouraged. I told people if I knew anything else to do, I'd give up painting . . . I'm very happy about where I am. I'm enjoying painting so much. I feel I have been successful.

William Halsey, 1996[46]

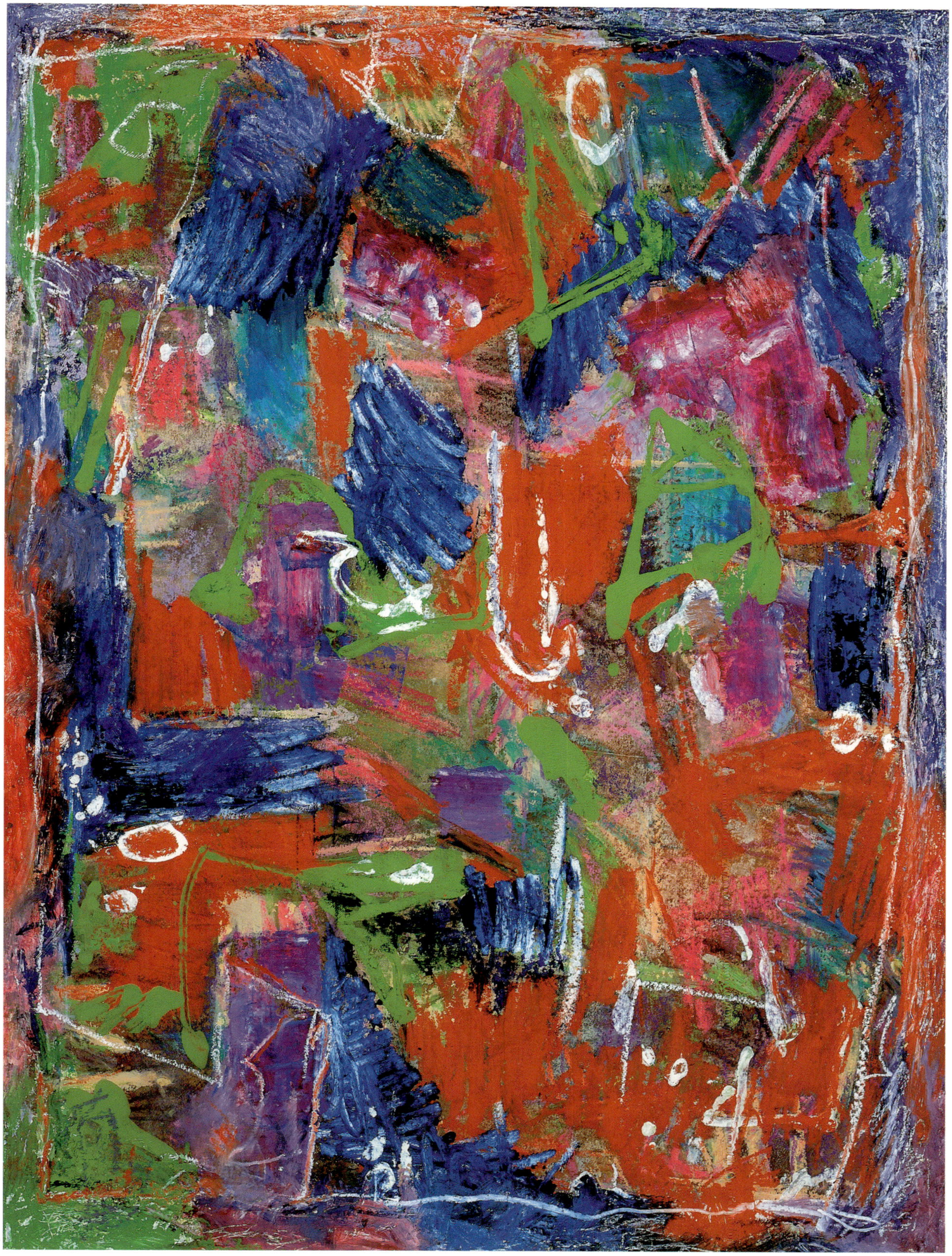

ENDNOTES

1 Halsey, artist's statement in "Changing Images: 1936-1987," exhibition sponsored by Piccolo Spoleto at Beth Elohim synagogue, 1987.

2 Verner to Halsey, 23 May 1934, Verner papers, South Carolina Historical Society, Charleston, South Carolina.

3 Halsey to Bragg, 11 August 1934, Bragg papers, South Carolina Historical Society.

4 Roberta A. Sheehan, "Boston Museum School, A Centennial History: 1876-1976" (Ph.D. dissertation, Boston College, 1983), 139-142.

5 Interview with the author, 1 April 1998.

6 Letter to the author, January, 1999.

7 Halsey quoted in Angela D. Mack, *Merton D. Simpson: The Journey of an Artist* (Charleston: Gibbes Museum of Art, 1995), unpaginated.

8 Simpson to the author, 12 December 1998.

9 Interview with the author, 1 April 1998.

10 Rutenberg to the author, 13 December 1998.

11 Kowalski to the author, 6 January 1999.

12 Interview with the author, 1 April 1998.

13 Halsey, artist's statement, "Changing Images."

14 Interview with the author, 24 October 1998.

15 Interview with the author, 1 April 1998.

16 Roberta Kefalos, *William Halsey and Corrie McCallum: Now and Then* (Charleston: Gibbes Museum of Art, 1989), unpaginated.

17 William Halsey, "Mural Painting in South Carolina," *South Carolina Magazine*, January 1953, 16.

18 Interview with the author, 1 April 1998.

19 Halsey quoted in Margaret Harold, *Oil Paintings and Why They Won the Prize* (Nashville: Allied Publications, Inc., 1960), 40.

20 Interview with the author, 1 April 1998.

21 Lane F. Beamer, "What Does A Butterfly Represent?" *Sandlapper*, September 1968; and interview with the author, 24 October 1998.

22 Interview with the author, 1 April 1998.

23 Alonzo Lansford, *Art Digest*, July 1948, and Robert M. Coates, *New Yorker*, 2 June 1951.

24 Carlyle Burrows, *The New York Herald Tribune*, 27 May 1951.

25 Anthony F. Janson, "William Halsey," *Art Voices/South*, April 1978.

26 Artist's statement, "William Halsey: Recent Work 1990-1994," College of Charleston, 1995.

27 "Artistic Tradition," *Gateway Magazine*, February 1958.

28 Halsey, artist's statement, circa 1968, Halsey archives.

29 Interview with the author, October 1998.

30 Robert Marks, "William Halsey–Perspective and Retrospective," College of Charleston, 1977.

31 Halsey quoted in Harold, *Oil Paintings*.

32 Interviews with the author, March and October 1998.

33 Janson, "William Halsey."

34 "Stones of Time," Spoleto Festival exhibition brochure, 1982.

35 Halsey, artist's statement, circa 1982, Halsey archives.

36 Interview with the author, October 1998.

37 Halsey quoted in Nancy Smith, "Abstract Art Show Features Three Distinct Approaches," *News and Courier*, 6 April 1980.

38 Halsey quoted in Harold, *Oil Paintings*.

39 Halsey quoted in Beamer, "What Does A Butterfly Represent?"

40 Mark Sloan, "William Halsey: Recent Work 1990-1994," College of Charleston, 1995.

41 Interview with the author, October 1998.

42 Nicholas Drake, "Halsey's Passion for Art Shows Zeal of Commitment," *Post and Courier*, March 12, 1995.

43 Halsey, artist's statement, circa 1982, Halsey archives.

44 Halsey, artist's statement, School of the Arts, College of Charleston, 1994.

45 Halsey, quoted in Gale Young, "Halsey in Review," *Charleston Evening Post*, 27 October 1972.

46 Halsey quoted in Jeffrey Day, "Painting Boldly into the Twilight," *The State*, 8 December 1996.

Chronology

1915:
Born, Charleston, South Carolina

1928-1931:
Studies with Elizabeth O'Neill Verner at the Charleston Museum and accompanies her on sketching trips around the city; meets Edward I. R. Jennings and studies with him briefly

1932:
Graduates from Charleston High School and enters University of South Carolina in Columbia

1934 and 1935:
Studies in Boothbay Harbor, Maine, and with Margaret Moore Walker in Greenville

1934:
Leaves the University of South Carolina

1935-1939:
Studies at the Boston Museum School of Fine Arts under Alexandre Iaocvleff, Karl Zerbe, and Lewis Rubinstein; in his final year teaches fresco

1939-1941:
After marrying Corrie McCallum in June 1939, travels to Mexico on a Paige Fellowship from the Boston Museum School

1939:
First one-man exhibition at the Berkshire Museum, Pittsfield, Massachusetts

1940:
Gibbes Art Gallery mounts a solo exhibition that subsequently travels to Norfolk Museum and Lynchburg Art Gallery in Virginia

1941-1942:
Resides in Charleston and teaches privately

1942:
One-man exhibition at the Telfair Academy in Savannah

1942-1945:
Lives in Savannah while serving as director of the School of the Telfair Academy; during the latter years of the war works in Savannah shipyards

1945:
Moves to Charleston; works as director of art classes at the Gibbes Art Gallery

1948-1953:
Exhibits with Bertha Schaefer Gallery in New York

1953-1964:
With Corrie McCallum and Willard Hirsch, founds and conducts the Charleston Art School

1958:
Exhibits at the Clemson College of Architecture

1960:
Begins his extensive annual travel regimen that ultimately includes: the Yucatan, Guatemala, Honduras, Colombia, Ecuador, Peru, Portugal, Spain, Morocco, Oaxaca, France, Italy, England, Greece, Yugoslavia, Tanzania, Rwanda, Kenya, Tahiti, Samoa, and the Galapagos Islands

1965-1984:
Teaches at the College of Charleston

1967:
Recent Paintings by Corrie McCallum and William Halsey at the Mint Museum of Art, Charlotte

1971:
Publishes *A Travel Sketchbook* with Corrie McCallum

1972:
Greenville County Museum of Art organizes a major retrospective exhibition that circulates to the Gibbes Art Gallery, the Florence Museum, and the Columbia Museum of Art; accompanied by the volume, *William M. Halsey: Retrospective*, by Jack A. Morris, Jr.

1976:
Issues *Mayan Journal*, combining commentary with sketches

1982:
Stones of Time exhibition at the South Carolina State Ports Authority, Spoleto Exhibition

1983:
Moroccan Landscapes and Fragments exhibition at the Simons Center for the Arts, College of Charleston

1983-1985:
Painting in the South: 1564-1980, a touring exhibition organized by Virginia Museum of Art, includes two examples of his work

1984:
After twenty years, retires from the College of Charleston, where the gallery at the Simons Fine Arts Center is named in his honor

1987:
Changing Images, an exhibition sponsored by Piccolo Spoleto, is held at Beth Elohim Synagogue

1989:
Now and Then: William Halsey and Corrie McCallum, a joint exhibition, is organized by the Gibbes Museum of Art

1995:
The College of Charleston awards the artist an honorary degree

1995:
William Halsey: Recent Work 1990-1994, exhibited at the Halsey Gallery, College of Charleston

1996:
Hampton III Gallery, Greenville, exhibits recent works of art on paper

1999:
Dies in Charleston

Checklist

(Unless otherwise noted all works are from the collection of the artist; in all measurements, height precedes width)

Night Houses, 1951
oil on Masonite
19 1/2 x 23 3/4 inches
(illustrated on page 21)

End of Town, 1953
casein on Masonite
20 1/2 x 43 inches
Collection of the Columbia Museum of Art, Columbia, Museum purchase, Third Annual Guild of South Carolina Artists Show, Purchase Award
(illustrated on page 23)

Blue Grille, 1956
oil on Masonite
34 x 24 inches
Collection of the College of Charleston
(illustrated on page 25)

From Outer Space, 1964
wood, metal, and wire
31 x 12 x 11-3/4 inches
Collection of the Greenville County Museum of Art, Museum purchase
(illustrated on page 27)

Voodoo, Violet, and Blue, 1965
oil on wood
39 x 21 inches
(illustrated on page 29)

Andalusia, 1966
oil on wood and paper on plywood
48 x 24 inches

Baby's First Step, 1966
wood and mixed media
28 x 12 x12 inches

Sea Monument, 1966
wood
46 x 9 1/2 x 8 3/4 inches
(illustrated on page 37)

White Counterpoint, 1966
oil on wood,
33 x 32 x 3 inches
(illustrated on page 31)

Black Chair II, 1968
oil on Masonite
48 x 32 inches
Collection of the Greenville County Museum of Art, gift of the artist
(illustrated on page 39)

Red Orbit, 1969
collage on Masonite
42 x 48 inches
(illustrated on page 33)

From Darkness, 1970
oil/collage on Masonite
36 x 48 inches

Red Earth, Yellow Moon, 1970
oil/collage on Masonite
48 x 48 inches
(illustrated on page 35)

Old Man, 1972
oil on Masonite
48 x 48 inches
Collection of Thomas H. Cooper
(illustrated on page 41)

Hanged Man, 1972/1973
oil on Masonite
71 /12 x 23 1/2 inches

Hanged Man, 1972/1973
oil on Masonite
71 1/2 x 23 1/2 inches

Hanged Men, 1972/1973
oil on Masonite
71 1/2 x 36 inches
(illustrated on page 43)

Stones of Time: Air, 1982
oil on Masonite,
96 x 48 inches
(illustrated on page 45)

Stones of Time: Fire, 1982
oil on Masonite
96 x 48 inches
(illustrated on page 47)

Stones of Time: Itzmina, 1982
oil on Masonite
96 x 48 inches
(illustrated on page 46)

Grandfather, 1985
oil on Masonite
72 x 45 x 2 inches

Two-faced Graffiti God #1, 1985
oil on Masonite
52 3/4 x 24 x 1 7/8 inches
(illustrated on pages 48-49)

Metamorphosis, 1985/1991/1998
oil-stick on Masonite
50 1/2 x 38 3/4 inches
(illustrated on page 77)

Double Congo Doors, 1986
oil/collage on hollow-core door
80 x 72 inches
(illustrated on page 51)

Moon Door, 1986
oil on hollow-core door
80 x 36 inches
(illustrated on page 54)

Shaman II, 1986
incised steel
60 x 12 x 1 1/4 inches
(illustrated on page 55)

Nail, Spike, and Copper Tube, 1987
wood and metal
28 x 24 x 4 1/2 inches
(illustrated on page 59)

Latch, Buckle and Key, 1987/1989
wood and metal
27 x 23 3/4 x 5 1/4 inches

Figura, 1988
oil/collage on hollow-core door
80 x 30 inches
Collection of Dr. and Mrs. Ambrose Hampton
(illustrated on page 53)

River Gods, 1988
oil on hollow-core doors
79 x 66 1/2 inches
Collection of Mae and Dennis Tavernetti
(illustrated on page 57)

Shaman, 1988
acrylic on hollow-core door
80 x 36 inches
(illustrated on page 61)

Totemic, 1989
acrylic on hollow-core door
80 x 36 inches
(illustrated on page 63)

Tantara, 1991
oil-stick on Masonite
50 5/8 x 38 3/8 inches
(illustrated on page 65)

Pavane with Sunlight, 1993
oil-stick on Masonite
50 x 38 1/2 inches
(illustrated on page 67)

Magic Carpet, 1994
acrylic/collage on Masonite
48 1/2 x 46 1/4 inches
(illustrated on page 69)

Denim, 1995
oil/collage on Masonite
48 x 48 1/4 inches
(illustrated on page 71)

Orbit, 1996
oil/collage on Masonite
48 x 48 inches
(illustrated on page 73)

Red Square, 1997
oil/collage on Masonite
46 1/4 x 48 1/4 inches
(illustrated on page 75)